This book belongs to:

_____

_____

Andrea Kösslinger · Sibylle Reiter

Mushrooms
Favorite Recipes

ACKNOWLEDGMENTS

The authors would like to thank Gabi Fischer, Dr. Zita Funkenhauser, Irene Kilian, Markus Klamert, Peter Koch, Helga Kößlinger, Kerstin and Richard Leicher from the Gasthaus Leicher in Oberfinning, Eva Matzke, Gertrud Reiter, and Marianne Schneider for valuable tips and recipes.

Published originally under the title Lieblingsrezepte mit Pilzen © 2004 Verlag W. Hölker GmbH, Münster. English translation for the U.S. market ©2005 Silverback Books, Inc.

Graphics: Niels Bonnemeier
Production: Patty Holden
Translator: Christie Tam
Project Editor: Lisa M. Tooker
Editors: Christiane Leesker, Lynda Zuber Sassi

ISBN 1-59637-014-9

Printed in China

CONTENTS

Unless otherwise indicated, all recipes make four servings.

GETTING IN THE MOOD

After a warm, late-summer rain, nature draws you out into the crisp, clear air. If you happen to take a walk in the woods, you'll find yourself beguiled by the soft, silky fragrance of flowers, moist earth, pine needles, moss, and mulch.

This is ideal climate for coaxing mushrooms out of the ground. So be quick about it, put on sturdy shoes, pick up your basket and mushroom knife, and head for the woods, the home of boletus mushrooms, morels, and bay boletes.

And, if your mushroom foraging is a success; here's what you can expect that evening: Fresh mushrooms tossed in butter, eaten out of the pan, accompanied by French bread, and a glass of wine. You'll close your eyes in ecstasy, take a deep breath, and think back on a beautiful day. There are many different kinds of mushrooms. They all taste best fresh, no doubt about it, but can also be preserved and enjoyed all year round. Some types of dried mushrooms are almost as tasty as fresh. Heavenly oils are infused with the rich aromas of intensely flavorful mushrooms. The Italian's are so crazy about their "funghi" that they make delicious pestos from porcini, truffles, cremini, and white mushrooms. Of course, this book will give you more than just Italian culinary secrets—we're offering you an international culinary experience.

Thank goodness a number of varieties are available as of late summer, including large cauliflower mushrooms, small honey mushrooms, scaly tooth, and horn of plenty mushrooms, which can be found in farmers' markets. If you can't take advantage of the wide variety available at the market, don't despair! Cultivated (oyster, white, cremini, and shiitake mushrooms) and prepackaged wild mushrooms can be found at most local specialty stores or supermarkets.

And now start swinging that wooden spoon! Turn the pages and "cook your way through." We're sure you'll have more than one favorite dish!

Have fun and bon appetite from

Andrea Kössling *Sibylle Reiter*

A TOUR OF THE WORLD
OF MUSHROOMS

What You Need to Know When Picking Mushrooms

Before you start picking mushrooms, familiarize yourself with the following important practices:

- When picking mushrooms, it's best to take a wicker- or woven-wood basket. Never use a plastic bag. Plastic bags cause the mushrooms to become slimy and the protein they contain starts to break down. Eating these mushrooms can cause toxic reactions!
- Keep your harvest well ventilated with fresh air.
- Trim the mushrooms with a knife before placing them in the basket.
- Cut mushrooms close to the ground only if you're sure of what they are. Otherwise, twist them out of the mycelium so you can also examine the base of the stem. Gather only mushrooms that you are absolutely familiar with. If you have even the shadow of a doubt, leave them alone!
- Always carry a well-illustrated identification book. Compare each individual point: Shape and color of the cap, stem, gills or pores, location, and time of year found, etc.
- Pick only as many mushrooms as you will use for a single meal (unless you want to freeze or dry them).
- Don't pick the small "buttons" that haven't yet released their spores.
- If you're still uncertain about what you've picked, take your mushrooms to the grocery store or local farmer's market and ask the experts to help you identify them.
- Never eat mushrooms that you are unsure about.

When you come home with your harvest, you can begin by cleaning the mushrooms immediately. Rinse them only as a last resort (e.g., if you aren't sure whether the place where you found them has been sprayed with pesticides). They soak up water instantly and lose flavor. It's best to clean them using a mushroom brush or paper towel, removing blemishes and hard or tough stems with a knife. If you don't want to process your mushrooms right away, freeze them immediately after cleaning and cutting them up. To prepare, place the mushrooms in a pot or pan while frozen so they don't become mushy.

A well-known but out-dated culinary rule says: "Never reheat mushrooms." Mushrooms are composed of water and a lot of protein—a combination that spoils easily. In the past when people didn't have refrigerators, this was a problem. Today, mushroom dishes can be reheated as long as they've been refrigerated after their first serving. But better safe than sorry—don't keep mushroom dishes for more than one day!

Mushroom Basics

We do not claim to give a complete selection of mushrooms here. Nor are these descriptions in any way meant to replace a good identification book. We've simply brought together all the varieties used in the recipes in this book. Some of them will only be familiar to you if you're "into mushrooms." Some are available in season from farmers' markets (chanterelles, boletus mushrooms, bay boletes, etc.), while others are cultivated mushrooms that can be found in supermarkets (white, cremini, and oyster mushrooms) or in gourmet shops (truffles). In recent years, Asian mushrooms such as shiitake and wood ear have arrived on our shores. They can be purchased in Asian markets or supermarkets, either fresh or dried.

Scaly Tooth Mushrooms (*Sarcodon imbricatus*) have an especially large, broad, beige cap covered with chocolate-brown scales and a relatively short stem. The scales on the cap are arranged in concentric circles around a depression in the center. On the underside of the caps are teeth that are white when young and later turn a grayish-brown. When older, these mushrooms taste bitter. Many people like to eat scaly tooth mushrooms whole, fried in batter, but they are also tasty cut into strips and sautéed. They are inedible raw and do not obtain their nutty flavor until they come in contact with warm butter. Scaly tooth mushrooms love conifer woods and grow from August to October.

●

Chanterelle Mushrooms (*Cantharellus cibarius*) are tasty gilled mushrooms that used to be very common, thus the old German saying, "That's not worth a chanterelle!" Air pollutants and the increased use of fertilizers and pesticides make it hard for chanterelles to grow. Chanterelles prefer the soil under conifers. Their caps can be up to 2⅓-inches wide, ranging in color from egg-yellow to orange. They are tapered at the base and then spread out into a funnel shape with wavy margins. The forked gills running up the stems are of the same color as the stems.

Horn of Plenty Mushrooms (*Craterellus cornucopioides*) are commonly referred to as **Trumpets of Death**, a somber name based on their grayish-black color and trumpet-like shape. The horn of plenty is one of the most delicious mushroom varieties. They can be found from August to October in mixed hard-wood forests, where they generally grow in large clusters. This little mushroom is only 2- to 4-inches high. The cap's funnel ends in wavy margins and the mushroom's flesh is thin. They are almost invisible. Gilled mushrooms are great for drying and are used either whole or ground up as a seasoning for soups and sauces. These mushrooms can be preserved for year-round use in the form of pesto. Fresh out of the pan, fried in plain butter, or in a risotto, they are an absolute delicacy.

King Boletes, **Porcini**, or **Cèpes** (*Boletus edulis*) are at home in higher altitudes, such as forests in mountainous areas. They have an unmistakable appearance. The caps of these tube mushrooms are 2- to 8-inches across, light to dark brown, with tubes on the underside that are white when young, and later turn yellowish to olive-green. The flesh of their club-shaped stems is firm and these mushrooms have a pleasantly nutty fragrance. They can be found from July to October in conifer and mixed forests. If you find one, its many offspring won't be far off. Boletus mushrooms belong to a large and delicious family. The Summer Bolete (*Boletus aestivalis*), the Queen Bolete (*Boletus aereus*), and the Pine Bolete (*Boletus pinophilus*) are also prized delicacies in the kitchen.

Bay Boletes (*Xerocomus badius*) are just as delicious as their cousins the boletus mushrooms. Their caps are brown to reddish-brown. The tubes are light yellow when young, later becoming yellow-green, and turning a bluish color when bruised. When cut, their flesh immediately becomes tinged with blue, but this coloring disappears when they're fried or sautéed. The stem is light to yellow-brown. In the case of older mushrooms, the tube layer will have become slightly slimy and should be removed before preparation. These delicious mushrooms are often found in large quantities from July to October in conifer and mixed forests.

Slippery Jack Mushrooms (*Suillus luteus*) are found from sea level to high in the mountains, preferring the soil under conifers. They are another tube mushroom and have a distinctive chocolate-brown and yellow-brown cap. The stems are translucent white with a purplish ring. The slimy skin on the cap is easy to remove. This can be done when they're picked or before preparation. The tube color is from yellow to olive-green. Slippery jacks spring up as early as June and can be harvested at higher altitudes into October.

Field or **Meadow Mushrooms** (*Agaricus campestris*) can often be found "in the wild." During a dry summer, a cloudburst or thunderstorm can cause large colonies to shoot up out of the ground. As the name indicates, they are found in meadows and pastures. Their caps are white to brownish. The gills of the young mushrooms are pink, later turning chocolate-brown. Their strong white stems have an extremely fragile ring. These mushrooms are now grown year-round as cultivated mushrooms (*Agaricus hortensis*) and are available in white, brown, or pink. They are the mushrooms most commonly used in our cuisine. They taste great raw, sautéed, baked, and preserved.

Honey Mushrooms (*Armillaria mellea*) generally grow in clusters on dead logs or living trees. Their caps are honey-yellow to brown and covered with brown-black, shaggy scales when young. The stems are yellow to brown with a web-like ring. Honey mushrooms are very common and are found throughout the fall both in and out of the woods. Be careful: They are poisonous raw and must always be sufficiently cooked. Many people experience an allergic reaction, so eat a small quantity the first time you try them. Some mushroom guides recommend boiling them and throwing away the cooking water before actually preparing them. The young caps are edible and tasty.

Parasol Mushrooms (*Macrolepiota procera*) can be found anywhere in well-lit forests from August to October. They sprout up at the edges of woods, in clearings, and in forest meadows. As typical tall-stemmed, gilled mushrooms, they have a broad, umbrella-like cap with a diameter of up to 15½ inches, chocolate-colored scales, and movable rings around their hollow stems. Small parasols are shaped like drumsticks. The caps of the giant parasols are delicious breaded and fried like cutlets, dried, grated, or preserved in oil.

Oyster Mushrooms (*Pleurotus ostreatus*) have a gray to brown cap. These large, fleshy, shell-shaped mushrooms grow from fall to December on the trunks of hardwood trees. Young oyster mushrooms have an especially distinctive odor. Generally, however, those used in our cuisine are the cultivated variety. They are lighter in color and are raised on mushroom farms without spores. Even people plagued by allergies can eat them. Oyster mushrooms are ideal breaded and fried. Usually, they are cut into strips and browned in a pan. Raw, they are tasteless.

Cauliflower Mushrooms (*Sparassis crispa*) resemble a natural sponge in their shape and color. Their proud dimensions can reach a width and height of 7¾–12 inches. The individual mushroom grows on a thick, deeply rooted stalk at the base of old conifers. Similar versions found on the roots of oak trees are relatives of the cauliflower mushroom, called "Hen of the Woods." Due to the cauliflower mushroom's large size, it also becomes quite heavy and often reaches a weight of 2¼–4½ lb. Before processing, rinse cauliflower mushrooms thoroughly (don't worry, despite their sponge-like appearance they don't soak up water). Then sauté in butter and add seasonings.

The extremely aromatic **Shiitake Mushrooms** (*Lentinus edodes*) are commonly known by their Japanese name, whereas their Chinese name, **Dong Gu** is less familiar. Their fine, nutty flavor has earned them the title "king of the mushrooms." Shiitakes are related to wood ear mushrooms. They grow on the bark of a certain type of oak tree and are used sparingly because of their intense flavor. Fresh shiitakes have a meaty brown cap and firm flesh. This type of mushroom can be used both fresh and dried.

Wood Ear Mushrooms (*Hirneola auricula judae*) have many other names, including **Mo-Er Mushrooms**, **Chinese Morels**, **Cloud Ear Mushrooms**, **Tree Ear Mushrooms**, and **Judas' Ear Mushrooms**. Their flat, uneven shape looks like an ear. These brown mushrooms grow on the trunks of beech, walnut, and elder trees. In Asian markets, they're mainly available dried. Before cooking, they need to be soaked in water. Be careful: These mushrooms can expand to five or six times their dry volume! Because they have little flavor of their own, they're ideal for giving dishes a far-eastern flair.

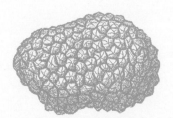

Their majesties, the **Truffles** (*Terrae tuffolae*), whether white or black, grow underground to sizes of up to 12 inches. Their hiding places are top secret. They prefer the roots of beech, lime, and elm trees, though oak and maple also make acceptable hosts. Sows and dogs are often used to sniff them out because they give off an animal scent of "testosterase," similar to the male hormone testosterone. Once a female animal catches a whiff of this odor, there's no holding her back. Humans are attracted less by their scent than by their flavor. If you miss the September-to-December truffle season, don't fret, truffles can still be found in your favorite gourmet shop.

SOUPS

Classic Cream of Mushroom Soup

1 small onion, ¾ lb white mushrooms, 2 tbs butter,
2 tbs dried vegetable stock, ½ cup white wine,
¾ cup heavy cream, Salt, Freshly ground white pepper,
Juice of ½ lemon, Chopped parsley for garnish

Peel onion and dice finely. Clean mushrooms with a mushroom brush or paper towel, trim, and slice. In a pot, melt butter, then braise onion until translucent. Add mushrooms and brown for about 2 minutes. Add stock, white wine, and cream, then simmer over low heat for about 10 minutes. Season soup with salt, pepper, and lemon juice to taste, then purée. Serve in warm soup bowls and garnish with chopped parsley.

Clear Bolete Soup

4 oz dried boletus mushrooms, 1 cup hot water, 1 large carrot,
2 green onions, 4 tsp instant mushroom soup mix,
Salt, Freshly ground pepper, Parsley or chervil leaves for garnish

Soak dried boletus mushrooms in hot water for 1 hour. Clean carrots, peel, and cut into fine diamond-shaped pieces. Clean green onions and chop into rings. In a pot, bring 4 cups water to a boil with instant mushroom soup mix. Add mushrooms, including soaking water, carrots, and green onions, then simmer for 5 minutes. Season with salt and pepper to taste. Transfer to warm soup cups and garnish with parsley or chervil leaves.

Even children love this soup; add some small star-shaped pasta to make it fun.

Cream of Pea Soup with Boletus Mushrooms

½ oz dried boletus mushrooms, 2 shallots, 2 tbs butter,
⅔ cup baby peas (fresh or frozen), 1 tsp sugar,
1 cup chicken stock, 1 cup heavy cream

Soak ⅓ oz mushrooms in hot water. Pulverize remaining mushrooms in a mortar. Peel shallots and cut into thin rings. In a saucepan, melt butter, then braise shallots until translucent. Add peas, dust with sugar, and braise briefly. Add chicken stock, ⅔ cup cream, and 3 tbs mushroom soaking water. Simmer for 2 minutes. Using a slotted spoon, remove some of the peas from the soup and set aside. Purée soup, put through a strainer, and reheat. Drain mushrooms, chop finely, and mix with peas. Whip remaining cream until semi-stiff and set aside 4 tbs. Add the rest of the cream to the soup and froth with a hand blender.

Pour mushroom-pea mixture in large cappuccino cups, then pour foamed soup over the top. Top each cup with 1 tbs semi-stiff cream and garnish with ground mushroom powder.

This "green cappuccino" makes an elegant appetizer. Fresh boletus mushrooms can be substituted for dried. In that case, use about 5 oz. For the "cocoa" on top, however, you must have dried!

Tuscan Mushroom Soup with Toasted Ciabatta

2 cloves garlic, 1 onion, 3 stalks celery, 2 beefsteak tomatoes,
3–4 medium porcini mushrooms (may substitute 9 oz cremini mushrooms),
2 stalks fresh thyme, 1 bunch chives, ¼ cup Parmigiano-Reggiano,
⅓ cup extra-virgin olive oil, 6 cups beef stock,
Salt, Freshly ground black pepper, 1 small ciabatta loaf

Peel garlic and mince. Peel onion and dice finely. Clean celery and dice. Cut an X through the skin on the tomatoes, blanch, peel, and remove seeds and cores. Chop tomato flesh coarsely. Clean mushrooms with a mushroom brush or paper towel, trim, and slice. Rinse thyme and chives and pat dry. Strip thyme leaves from stems and chop chives into small rings. Finely grate Parmigiano-Reggiano.

In a pot, heat olive oil, then sweat garlic and onion. Add celery and braise. Add stock and tomatoes. Season with thyme, salt, and pepper. Simmer over medium heat for about 20 minutes. Add mushrooms and simmer for another 10 minutes at the same temperature. Cut ciabatta into thin slices and toast. Place 2–3 slices in each soup bowl. Pour soup over the top and sprinkle with chives and grated Parmigiano-Reggiano.

This soup used to be a simple poor man's meal. It used whatever type of vegetable could be harvested. The well-known Italian minestrone probably had a similar origin.

Creamy Mushroom Soup
with Celery and Leek

⅔ cup celery, 1 medium leek,
14 oz slippery jack, scaly tooth, cremini, or white mushrooms,
2 tbs dried beef stock, 6 cups hot water, ¾ cup heavy cream,
3 tbs butter, Salt, Freshly ground pepper, 1 pinch grated nutmeg,
1–2 tbs crème fraîche, Nasturtium flowers for garnish

Cut celery stalks and leek in half, clean, rinse thoroughly, and cut into large pieces. Clean mushrooms with a mushroom brush or paper towel, trim (in the case of slippery jacks, peel caps), and cut into quarters. Dissolve dried stock in hot water. Whip cream until stiff, cover, and refrigerate. In a large pot, melt butter, then braise celery and leeks. Add stock. Add mushrooms, cover, and simmer over medium heat for 35–40 minutes, stirring occasionally. Season soup with salt, pepper, and nutmeg to taste. Purée with a hand blender. Stir in cream and beat thoroughly with a wire whisk. Transfer mushroom soup to bowls, place a dollop of crème fraîche in the center of each, garnish with several nasturtium flowers, and serve immediately.

Hungarian Mushroom Soup

9 oz boletus mushrooms, 1 small onion, 2 carrots, 1 parsley root,
3 tbs butter, 2 tbs flour, 1 tsp Hungarian sweet paprika,
4 cups beef stock, 3 tbs rice, 1 bunch parsley, ½ cup crème fraîche

Clean mushrooms with a mushroom brush or paper towel, trim, and cut into thin slices. Peel onion, carrots and parsley root, and dice finely. In a pot, melt butter then braise vegetables over low heat for about 5 minutes. Add flour and paprika and stir well. Add stock and rice. Simmer over medium heat for about 15 minutes until done. Rinse parsley, pat dry, remove leaves from stems, and chop finely. Enrich soup with crème fraîche; transfer to soup bowls and sprinkle with parsley just before serving.

Bavarian Mushroom Soup

14–16 oz boletus mushrooms, 2 onions, 2 cloves garlic,
2 bunches parsley, ¼ cup butter, 5–6 cups chicken or vegetable stock,
1 cup heavy cream, Salt, Freshly ground black pepper

Clean mushrooms with a mushroom brush or paper towel, trim, and slice. Peel onions and garlic and dice finely. Rinse parsley, pat dry, and remove leaves from stems.

In a pan, melt butter, then sweat onions and garlic. Add three-quarters of the mushrooms and braise briefly. Add approximately 1¼ cups stock. In a blender, purée pan contents and parsley (set aside 1 tbs for garnish), then pour into a pot. Add remaining stock and mushrooms. Simmer over low heat for about 30 minutes. Stir in cream, and season to taste with salt and pepper. Transfer to soup bowls, garnish with parsley, and serve.

Cream of Leek Soup with Bay Boletes

1 small leek, 1 small onion, 2 tbs dried vegetable stock,
6 cups hot water, ½ cup heavy cream,
8–10 bay boletes, ½ bunch Italian parsley,
3 tbs extra-virgin olive oil, ¼ cup dry white wine,
2 tbs Noilly Prat dry vermouth, 1 bay leaf,
2 tbs ice-cold butter, Salt, 1 pinch caraway powder,
2–3 drops Tabasco sauce, Butter for sautéing,
Freshly ground black pepper

Clean leek, rinse thoroughly, and cut into rings. Peel onion and dice finely. Dissolve dried stock hot water. Whip cream, cover, and refrigerate. Clean mushrooms with a mushroom brush or paper towel, trim, and cut into thin slices. Rinse parsley, pat dry, remove leaves from stems, and chop.

In a pot, heat olive oil, then braise leek and onion. Add wine and vermouth. Add bay leaf and stock. Cover and simmer over medium heat for about 30 minutes. Remove bay leaf and whisk in cream and butter. Do not return to a boil. Season with salt, caraway powder, and Tabasco to taste.

In a pan, melt butter, brown mushrooms lightly, and season with salt and pepper. Purée soup with a hand blender, transfer to warm soup bowls, garnish with mushrooms, and sprinkle with parsley.

Wild Mushroom and Spinach Soup

1 onion, 2 cloves garlic,
14 oz assorted wild mushrooms (e.g., boletus, bay boletes, field mushrooms),
1 potato, 2–3 stalks fresh thyme, ⅔ cup frozen spinach, 3 tbs butter,
4 cups canned chicken stock, Salt, Freshly ground black pepper,
Freshly grated nutmeg, ½ cup crème fraîche, 1 bunch parsley

Peel onion and garlic and dice finely. Clean mushrooms with a mushroom brush or paper towel, trim, and slice. Peel potatoes, rinse, and dice. Rinse thyme, pat dry, strip leaves from stems, and chop. Thaw spinach.

In a large pot, melt butter, then braise onion and garlic until translucent. Add mushrooms, potato, and thyme. Cover and simmer over medium heat for about 6 minutes. Add stock and spinach and stir well. Simmer for another 4–5 minutes. Purée soup and season with salt, pepper, and nutmeg to taste. Transfer to warm soup bowls, place a dollop of crème fraîche in the center, and garnish with parsley.

Potato Velouté with Fresh Boletus Mushrooms

¾ lb all-purpose potatoes, 2 cups beef stock,
¾ cup heavy cream, Salt, 2 green onions,
3–4 medium boletus mushrooms (about 8 oz),
3–4 stalks curly-leaved parsley, ⅓ cup softened butter,
3 tbs extra-virgin olive oil,
Freshly ground white pepper,
Freshly grated nutmeg

Peel potatoes, rinse, cut in half, and boil in a large amount of salted water. Combine stock and cream. Clean green onions and chop into fine rings. Clean mushrooms with a mushroom brush or paper towel, trim, and cut into thin slices. Rinse parsley, pat dry, remove leaves from stems, and chop finely. When the potatoes are done, drain, put through a ricer, and place in a bowl. Add butter and stock–cream mixture and stir into a smooth purée.

In a large pot, heat olive oil, then braise green onions. Add mushrooms and brown lightly. Season with salt and pepper. Remove a little of this mixture and set aside for garnish. Add potatoes to the pot and purée soup with a hand blender. Add more salt, pepper, and nutmeg to taste. Transfer to warm soup bowls, garnish with remaining mushroom–green onion mixture, and serve sprinkled with parsley.

 Never prepare potato purée with a hand blender—this will turn the potatoes into "paste" (use a ricer instead). Once there's enough liquid to make a soup, use a hand blender.

Potato Soup with Shiitake and Boletus Mushrooms

1 small leek, 1 green onion, 1 lb all-purpose potatoes,
5–6 fresh shiitake mushrooms, 2–3 slices white bread or baguette,
1 carrot, 1 small turnip, 1/4 oz dried boletus mushrooms,
3/4 cup heavy cream, 1 stalk marjoram, 1/2 bunch chives,
2 tbs extra-virgin olive oil, Salt, Freshly ground white pepper,
Freshly grated nutmeg, 1/4 cup butter, 1/4 cup dry white wine

Clean leek and green onion, rinse, and chop into fine rings. Peel potatoes, rinse, and dice finely. Clean shiitakes with a mushroom brush or paper towel, trim, and cut into thin strips. Toast white bread or baguette and dice. Clean carrot and turnip, peel, and dice finely. Crush dried boletus mushrooms in a mortar. In a small saucepan, combine boletus powder and cream. Rinse marjoram and chives, pat dry, and remove marjoram leaves from stems. Finely chop marjoram and chives.

In a pot, heat olive oil, then braise leek and green onion. Season with salt, pepper, and nutmeg to taste. Add 6 cups of water and cover. Simmer over medium heat for 30 minutes. In a pan, heat 2 tbs butter then sauté shiitakes and bread cubes until golden-brown. In a saucepan, melt remaining butter, then add carrot, and turnip. Season with salt and pepper. Add wine, cover, and cook for about 5 minutes until al dente.

In the meantime, heat cream and powdered boletus mushroom and let bubble up briefly. Using a hand blender, purée potato soup. Stir in boletus-cream mixture and cooked vegetables. Transfer to warm soup bowls, garnish with croutons and shiitakes, and sprinkle liberally with marjoram and chives. Serve immediately.

This soup is worth the effort. Its flavor is simply fantastic!

Asian "Good Morning Soup"

1 handful dried shiitake mushrooms,
1 handful dried sengiri daikon (health food stores or Asian markets),
2 carrots, 2 onions, ¾ inch fresh ginger root,
2 small leeks, ¼ cup soy sauce

Soak mushrooms and daikon in warm water for 2 hours. Clean and dice carrots. Peel and chop onions. In a large pot, combine mushrooms, daikon, carrots, and onions, including soaking water, then add 4 cups of water. Bring to a boil and simmer for 10 minutes. Peel ginger and mince. Clean leeks, rinse, and cut into strips. Add ginger and leeks to soup. Simmer over low heat until leeks are cooked but still firm. Season liberally to taste with soy sauce.

 This soup can be prepared several days in advance and served for breakfast. Of course, it can be eaten at other times, too.

Asian Soup with Chicken and Wood Ear Mushrooms

1 handful dried wood ear mushrooms, 3 baby carrots,
1 white onion, 1¼–1½ inch fresh ginger root, 1⅓ cup broccoli,
¼ Chinese cabbage, ⅔ lb chicken breast fillet,
Salt, Freshly ground black pepper, 3 tbs sesame oil,
6 cups chicken stock, 1½ tbs chopped cilantro, Soy sauce,
1 pinch cayenne pepper, Juice of ½ lemon, Cilantro leaves for garnish

Soak wood ear mushrooms in hot water for 20 minutes. Clean carrots, peel, and slice finely. Peel onion and cut into eighths. Peel ginger and chop very finely. Clean broccoli and separate into small florets. Clean Chinese cabbage and cut into strips the width of a finger. Rinse chicken breast, pat dry, and rub with salt and pepper.

In a pan, heat sesame oil then sear chicken on both sides. Reduce heat and continue sautéing until done. Remove from pan, let cool slightly, and cut into narrow strips.

Remove mushrooms from soaking water, rinse, drain, and cut into narrow strips. Heat stock. Cook carrots, onions, and broccoli in stock for 5 minutes. Add Chinese cabbage and simmer briefly. Add wood ear mushrooms, chicken strips, and cilantro. Season with soy sauce, cayenne pepper, and lemon juice to taste. Transfer soup to bowls, sprinkle with cilantro leaves, and serve immediately.

Hearty Chicken Soup with Wood Ear Mushrooms, Glass Noodles, and Chinese Vegetables

⅓ lb glass noodles, 1 handful dried wood ear mushrooms,
1 clove garlic, ¾ inch fresh ginger root, 1 small red chile pepper,
⅔ cup broccoli, ½ cup fresh bean sprouts, ½ cup canned bamboo shoots,
3 medium chicken breast fillets, 1 stalk fresh cilantro,
2 tbs dried chicken stock, 4 cups hot water, 3 tbs butter,
Salt, 1 tsp curry powder

Place glass noodles and wood ear mushrooms in separate containers. Pour boiling water over the top of each, and soak for 5 minutes. Drain glass noodles and transfer to Chinese soup bowls. Rinse mushrooms, trim hard portions, cut coarsely into strips, and add to glass noodles. Peel garlic and ginger and mince. Cut chile pepper in half, remove stem, seeds and interiors, and cut into thin slices. Clean broccoli and separate into florets. Rinse bean sprouts and bamboo shoots and drain. Cut bamboo shoots into narrow strips. Rinse chicken, pat dry, and cut into narrow strips. Rinse cilantro, pat dry, and remove leaves from stems.

Dissolve dried stock in hot water. Add garlic and ginger and let stand. In a pot, melt butter and lightly brown chicken. Season with salt and curry then add to stock. Add broccoli and bamboo shoots. Simmer for another 8 minutes. Add salt to taste. Add bean sprouts and chile pepper, bring to a boil, and immediately pour over the glass noodles and mushrooms in the bowls. Garnish with cilantro leaves and serve hot.

 Serve this soup with lemon wedges for squeezing over the top.

SALADS

Arugula Salad with Papaya and Slippery Jack Mushrooms

1 cup arugula, 1 papaya, Juice of ½ lemon, 3 tbs extra-virgin olive oil,
3 tbs balsamic vinegar, ½ tsp herb salt, Freshly ground black pepper,
3 large slippery jack mushrooms, 1 small onion,
1 clove garlic, Butter for sautéing, Salt

Rinse arugula, spin dry, and remove large stems. Cut papaya in half, remove seeds, peel, and cut into thin slices.

Combine lemon juice, olive oil, balsamic vinegar, herb salt, and pepper to make a dressing. Clean mushrooms with a mushroom brush or paper towel, trim (peeling the caps), and cut into strips that are not too fine. Peel onion and garlic and mince. In a pan, melt butter then braise onion and garlic until translucent. Add mushrooms and brown. Season with salt and pepper. Toss arugula with part of the dressing and arrange on large plates. Top with papaya slices and sautéed mushrooms. Drizzle with remaining dressing and serve immediately. Delicious with a fresh baguette.

Refreshing Mushroom Salad with Lime Dressing and Fig Crowns

Juice of 2 limes, ⅓ cup extra-virgin olive oil,
½ cup white balsamic vinegar, 2 tbs honey,
3 tbs evaporated milk, Salt, Freshly ground white pepper,
12 oz prince mushrooms, 4 fresh figs

Combine lime juice, olive oil, vinegar, honey, evaporated milk, salt, and pepper to make a dressing and marinate for several minutes.

Clean mushrooms with a mushroom brush or paper towel, trim, cut into thin slices, and arrange on large plates. Remove stems from figs and cut an X through each one from the top end almost to the bottom. Set figs like a crown on top of the mushrooms, bending the quarters outward slightly so the fruit sits stably on the mushrooms. In a small saucepan, heat dressing. Pour lukewarm dressing over the mushroom salad and figs.

Serve with fresh ciabatta and a glass of cold Prosecco. It's a great starter for a summery Italian meal!

Mâche Salad with Sautéed Oyster Mushrooms

1½ cups mâche, Juice of ½ lemon, ¼ cup canola oil,
¼ cup balsamic vinegar, ½ tsp herb salt,
Freshly ground white pepper, 10 ½ oz oyster mushrooms,
1 red onion, 2 cloves garlic, Butter for sautéing, Salt

Rinse mâche thoroughly and spin dry. Combine lemon juice, canola oil, balsamic vinegar, herb salt, and pepper to make a dressing. Clean mushrooms with a mushroom brush or paper towel, trim, and cut strips that are not too fine. Peel onion and garlic and mince. In a pan, melt butter then brown mushrooms, onion, and garlic. Season with salt and pepper. Carefully toss mâche and dressing. Arrange on large individual plates and top with sautéed mushrooms.

In a small, ungreased pan, toast 1 handful pine nuts until golden and sprinkle over the warm mushrooms.

When browning the oyster mushrooms, add 3 tbs walnut oil. It intensifies the nutty flavor of the mushrooms and goes well with the garlic.

Romaine Salad with Cheddar and Sautéed Chanterelles

7 oz chanterelle mushrooms, 1 green onion,
½–⅔ cup cheddar cheese (or tangy Swiss cheese),
1 large head romaine lettuce, 2 tbs butter,
Salt, Freshly ground black pepper, 2 tbs grapeseed oil,
2 tbs white wine vinegar, 2 tbs plain yogurt,
1 tsp brown sugar, 1 pinch cinnamon, ½ tsp herb salt

Clean chanterelles with a mushroom brush or paper towel and trim. Cut large mushrooms in half. Clean green onion and chop into fine rings. Grate cheese coarsely. Rinse lettuce, spin dry, and cut into strips the width of a finger. In a pan, melt butter then brown mushrooms on all sides. Season with salt and pepper. Combine grapeseed oil, green onion, vinegar, yogurt, sugar, and cinnamon to make a dressing. Season with herb salt and pepper. Carefully toss romaine lettuce and dressing and arrange on large plates. Sprinkle with cheese, top with warm chanterelles, and serve immediately.

For garnish, sprinkle freshly chopped parsley around the borders of the plates.

Warm Spinach Salad with Assorted Mushrooms and Yogurt Dressing

1 cup fresh spinach, 5 oz cremini mushrooms,
3½ oz white mushrooms, 5 oz cooked ham,
2 tbs Dijon mustard, ⅔ cup Greek yogurt,
½ cup heavy cream, 2 leeks, 1 clove garlic, 3 tbs canola oil,
Salt, Freshly ground black pepper, 2 tbs sherry,
½ cup dry white wine, 2 tbs capers

Clean spinach, rinse thoroughly, remove long stems, and pat dry. Clean mushrooms with a mushroom brush or paper towel, trim, and slice. Dice ham. Combine mustard, yogurt, and cream to make a dressing. Marinate for several minutes. Clean leeks, rinse, and cut into fine strips. Peel garlic and dice finely. In a large pan, heat oil, then braise leeks and garlic. Add mushrooms, season with salt and pepper, and sauté for 5 minutes. Add sherry and white wine and simmer over medium heat for another 5 minutes. Fold in spinach and wilt. Stir in dressing, ham, and capers. Marinate for 5 minutes. Season to taste with salt and pepper then transfer to individual plates.

 This dish is very quick to prepare, always successful, and tastes absolutely delicious with new potatoes.

Mushroom Fennel Salad

9 oz very small white mushrooms, 1 tbs butter, 2 fennel bulbs,
2 tbs balsamic vinegar, 2 tbs extra-virgin olive oil,
Salt, Freshly ground black pepper, ½ bunch parsley

Clean mushrooms with a mushroom brush or paper towel and trim. In a pan, melt butter and sauté mushrooms for about 5 minutes. Let cool. In the meantime, clean fennel bulbs and cut into thin slices. Combine mushrooms and fennel in a bowl.

Combine balsamic vinegar, olive oil, salt and pepper to make a marinade, and toss with mushrooms and fennel. Rinse parsley, pat dry, remove leaves from stems, and chop. Stir into salad, marinate for 30 minutes, and serve.

This salad keeps for several days in the refrigerator. In the summer, add cherry tomatoes for a little color.

Salad with Mushrooms and Bacon

¼ cup canola oil, 3 tbs white balsamic vinegar, 1 tbs maple syrup,
Salt, Freshly ground black pepper, 7 oz white mushrooms,
3½–5 oz horn of plenty mushrooms, ⅓ lb bacon,
1 head oak leaf lettuce, ½ bunch arugula, 1 head red leaf lettuce

Combine canola oil, balsamic vinegar, syrup, salt, and pepper to make a dressing. Cover and marinate in the refrigerator. Clean all mushrooms with a mushroom brush or paper towel and trim. Cut white mushrooms into thin slices. Dice bacon coarsely. Rinse oak leaf lettuce, arugula and red leaf lettuce, and spin dry and remove large stems.

Starting in a cold cast-iron pan, heat bacon and fry with horn of plenty mushrooms until crispy while stirring constantly (do not season). Arrange lettuce on large appetizer plates and drizzle with part of the dressing. Spread white mushrooms over the lettuce. Add remaining dressing to the pan of bacon and horns of plenty. Stir together and pour lukewarm pan contents over the lettuce. Season to taste with pepper and serve immediately.

Tastes best with an ice-cold beer or a well-chilled dry white wine.

Asian Rice Salad with Crabmeat

½ cup jasmine or basmati rice, 1 pinch salt,
1 handful fresh shiitake mushrooms, 1 oz fresh bean sprouts,
½ cucumber, ⅓ lb fresh crabmeat, 1 green onion,
¾ inch fresh ginger root, 3 tbs rice vinegar,
1 tsp soy oil, 1 tsp sesame oil, 2 tbs soy sauce, 1 tsp sugar

Cook rice in salted water according to directions. Clean mushrooms with a mushroom brush or paper towel, trim, and cut into thin slices. Rinse bean sprouts thoroughly and pat dry. Peel cucumber and slice with a vegetable slicer or mandolin. Cut crabmeat diagonally into pieces. Clean green onion and chop into fine rings. Peel and grate ginger. Combine rice vinegar, soy oil, sesame oil, soy sauce, and sugar to make a dressing. Stir in green onion and ginger.

Arrange rice, mushrooms, bean sprouts and cucumbers on large plates, and drizzle liberally with dressing. Garnish with crabmeat.

This salad is truly low-calorie. If you want it to be totally Asian, serve it with shrimp chips (krupuk). It's also great with sesame flatbread.

Fall Salad with Arugula, Sautéed Mushrooms, and Mozzarella

Juice of 1 lemon, ⅓ cup extra-virgin olive oil,
⅓ cup balsamic vinegar, 2 tbs maple syrup,
Herb salt, Freshly ground black pepper, 2 bunches arugula,
7 oz chanterelle, slippery jack, or shiitake mushrooms,
2 mozzarella cheese balls, Olive oil for sautéing

Combine lemon juice, oil, vinegar, syrup, herb salt, and pepper to make a dressing and marinate.

Rinse arugula, pat dry, and remove long stems. Clean mushrooms with a mushroom brush or paper towel, trim (peel caps of slippery jacks), and cut into thin slices. Dice mozzarella coarsely. In a pan, heat oil then brown mushrooms on all sides. Arrange arugula and mozzarella on a large platter, top with mushrooms, and drizzle liberally with dressing.

This salad is ideal for parties. Wait to drizzle the dressing until you're ready to start the buffet so the arugula will stay crispy.

Bread Salad with Wild Mushrooms, Bacon, and Eggs

2 cloves garlic, ⅔ cup extra-virgin olive oil,
8–10 slices crusty white bread, 12 oz assorted wild mushrooms,
1 bunch arugula, 1 head frisée lettuce, Juice of 1 lemon,
1 tsp brown sugar, 1 tsp Dijon mustard,
Herb salt, Freshly ground pepper, 10–12 slices bacon,
4 large eggs, Cress for garnish

Peel garlic, squeeze through a press, and mix well with half the olive oil. Preheat oven to 400°F. Cut bread into coarse cubes, drizzle with garlic oil, and bake in the oven on a baking sheet lined with parchment paper until golden. Clean mushrooms with a mushroom brush or paper towel, trim, and cut into quarters. Rinse arugula, pat dry, and remove large stems. Rinse frisée lettuce and pat dry. Cut large leaves in half.

Combine lemon juice, remaining olive oil, sugar, mustard, herb salt, and pepper to make a dressing. Carefully toss arugula, frisée and dressing, and arrange on salad plates. Top with toasted garlic bread. Starting in a cold cast-iron pan, heat bacon and sauté on all sides until golden. Add mushrooms and continue frying with bacon, stirring constantly. Soft boil eggs for about 4 minutes, plunge immediately into ice water, peel, and cut in half. Top lettuce with bacon and mushrooms, and garnish with eggs and cress. Serve immediately.

APPETIZERS & SNACKS

Mushroom Toast

7 oz white mushrooms, 1 small onion, ½ bunch parsley,
2 tbs butter, Salt, Freshly ground black pepper,
4 slices white sandwich bread, 4 slices Gouda

Preheat oven to 350°F. Clean mushrooms with a mushroom brush or paper towel, trim, and cut into thin slices. Peel onion and dice finely. Rinse parsley, pat dry, remove leaves from stems, and chop finely. In a pan, melt half the butter then braise onion. Add mushrooms and braise. Season with salt and pepper to taste. Toast bread and spread with remaining butter. Spread mushroom mixture on toast and top 1 slice Gouda. Brown in the oven for 8–10 minutes. Just before serving, sprinkle with parsley.

Truffle Omelet

Serves 2:
4 large eggs, Salt, Freshly ground white pepper,
2 tbs butter, About 1½ oz white truffles

Whisk 2 eggs with salt and pepper. In a pan, melt half the butter and cook eggs over low heat for 5 minutes until set. Slide omelet onto a plate, fold in half, and keep warm. Repeat this process to make a second omelet. Slice truffles over both and serve immediately.

Placing truffles in a jar with raw eggs and uncooked rice for 1 week, will transfer the truffle aroma to the eggs. An omelet made from these eggs will taste absolutely delicious!

Beef and Cremini Carpaccio

4¼ oz cremini mushrooms, ⅓ lb carpaccio, ¼ cup Parmigiano-Reggiano,
½–⅔ cup extra-virgin olive oil, Juice of ½ lemon,
½ tsp salt, Freshly ground black pepper

Clean mushrooms with a mushroom brush or paper towel, trim, and cut into thin slices (preferably with a truffle slicer, or an egg slicer will also work well). Arrange beef slices on large individual plates in a fan pattern and spread finely sliced mushrooms on top. Using a potato or vegetable peeler, shave Parmigiano-Reggiano thinly over the carpaccio. Combine olive oil, lemon juice, salt and pepper to make a dressing, and drizzle on top. Marinate briefly and serve with fresh ciabatta.

Grate zest from the lemon and use it as garnish around the rims of the plates.

Giant Stuffed Mushrooms

8 prince mushrooms, Juice of ½ lemon, 1 small onion,
1 clove garlic, 1½ oz smoked bacon, ½ bunch parsley, 1 tbs butter,
1½ tsp dried vegetable stock, ⅓ cup heavy cream, 2 tbs Boursin cheese,
Freshly ground pepper, ¼ cup grated Parmigiano-Reggiano,
Butter for the casserole dish

Preheat oven to 400°F. Clean mushrooms with a mushroom brush or paper towel and trim. Cut off stems, dice stems finely, and set aside. Immediately drizzle caps with lemon juice. Peel onion and chop. Peel garlic and squeeze through a press. Dice bacon finely. Rinse parsley, pat dry, remove leaves, and chop.

In a pan, melt butter then braise onion and garlic until translucent. Add bacon and mushroom stems and braise. Add dried stock, cream, Boursin, and parsley. Bring to a boil and season with pepper. Spoon mixture into mushroom caps and sprinkle with Parmigiano-Reggiano. Place caps in a greased casserole dish and brown in the oven for 12–15 minutes.

These stuffed mushrooms look fantastic when served on crispy mâche lettuce.

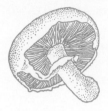

Crostini with Mushroom and Liver

2 shallots, 2 cloves garlic, 12 oz white mushrooms,
⅓ lb chicken liver, 1 handful fresh herbs (e.g., sage, thyme, parsley),
3 tbs extra-virgin olive oil, ½ cup canned veal stock,
Salt, Freshly ground black pepper, 1 tbs balsamic vinegar, 1 baguette

Preheat oven to 350°F. Peel shallots and garlic and mince. Clean mushrooms with a mushroom brush or paper towel and trim. Cut 2 mushrooms into paper-thin slices and set aside for garnish. Dice remaining mushrooms. Rinse chicken liver and pat dry. Rinse herbs, pat dry, and remove leaves from stems. Set aside some leaves for garnish and chop the rest.

In a pan, heat olive oil then braise diced shallots, garlic, and mushrooms for about 3 minutes. Add liver and brown. Add veal stock and bring to a boil. Stir in chopped herbs. Reduce heat to low until the mixture thickens. Season with salt, pepper, and balsamic vinegar.

Cut baguette into slices of equal thickness and toast in the preheated oven on a baking sheet lined with parchment paper until golden. Spread baguette slices with mushroom-liver mixture. Garnish with herbs and mushroom slices and serve immediately.

Spinach and Mushroom Gratin

1¾ cups frozen spinach, 1 small onion, 7 oz white mushrooms,
¼ cup butter, Butter for the casserole dish,
Salt, Freshly ground pepper, ⅓ cup heavy cream,
1½ tbs Noilly Prat dry vermouth,
2 tbs instant hollandaise sauce mix,
½ cup Gorgonzola mascarpone cheese

Thaw spinach. Peel onion and dice finely. Clean mushrooms with a mushroom brush or paper towel, trim, and slice. Preheat oven to 400°F. In a pan, melt half the butter and sauté onions until translucent. Add spinach and heat while stirring until the spinach has thawed completely. Season with salt and pepper. Transfer to a lightly greased casserole dish and smooth out the surface. Brown mushrooms in remaining butter, season with salt and pepper, then spread on top of the spinach. In the same pan, heat cream and Noilly Prat. Reduce slightly. Remove from heat and stir in hollandaise sauce mix. Return pan to the burner and return to a boil. Pour sauce over spinach and mushrooms. Chop cheese and sprinkle over the top. Brown under the oven broiler for 8–10 minutes.

 This dish is ideal as a vegetarian entrée (serves 2) or as a side dish with fish or poultry. You can also replace the Gorgonzola mascarpone with about ¼ cup Parmigiano-Reggiano.

Zucchini and Mushrooms

1 lb zucchini, 2 onions, 16 oz white mushrooms,
⅓–½ cup extra-virgin olive oil, Salt, Freshly ground pepper,
1–2 tbs dried vegetable stock, ¼ cup balsamic vinegar

Clean zucchini and cut into slices ½-inch thick. Peel and dice onions. Clean mushrooms with a mushroom brush or paper towel, trim, and cut into quarters. In a pan, heat ¼ cup olive oil, then brown zucchini and onions. Season with salt, pepper, and vegetable stock. Add mushrooms and sauté. Finally, add remaining olive oil and vinegar. Serve hot or cold with fresh bread.

Antipasto with Cremini and Porcini Mushrooms

2 cloves garlic, 7 oz cremini mushrooms,
3–4 medium porcini mushrooms, 3 stalks oregano,
3 stalks basil, 1 stalk rosemary, 2 tbs Parmigiano-Reggiano,
3 tbs butter, Herb salt, Freshly ground black pepper, ¼ cup dry white wine

Peel garlic and squeeze through a press. Clean mushrooms with a mushroom brush or paper towel. Cut cremini into quarters and porcini into thin slices. Rinse herbs and pat dry. Remove oregano and basil leaves from stems and cut coarsely into strips. Remove rosemary leaves from stems. Using a vegetable peeler, coarsely shave Parmigiano-Reggiano.

In a large pan, melt butter, then braise garlic. Add mushrooms and brown. Season with herb salt and pepper. Add white wine, cover, and simmer for 5 minutes. Stir in oregano and basil. Transfer mixture to an earthenware bowl. Add salt and pepper to taste. Sprinkle with rosemary and shaved Parmigiano-Reggiano. Cover and let stand for at least 2 hours.

 This antipasto tastes best with cold Prosecco and fresh focaccia or olive ciabatta.

Sautéed Mushrooms à la Toscana
with Garlic and Lemon

16 oz fresh mushrooms (e.g., cremini, bay boletes,
chanterelles, porcini, or a combination),
4 cloves garlic, ½ bunch curly-leaved parsley,
½ cup extra-virgin olive oil, 1 tbs butter, Juice of ½ lemon,
¼ cup tomato paste, Salt, Freshly ground white pepper

Clean mushrooms with a mushroom brush or paper towel, trim, and cut in half. Slice larger mushrooms. Peel garlic and cut into very thin slices. Rinse parsley, pat dry, remove large stems, and chop coarsely.

Preheat oven to 400°F. In a large pan, heat half the olive oil and brown half the mushrooms on all sides. Remove and keep warm. Repeat this process with the remaining oil and mushrooms. In the same pan, melt butter then braise garlic. Add lemon juice. Stir in tomato paste and season with salt and pepper. Return warm mushrooms to the pan and mix well with sauce. Add parsley, salt, and pepper to taste. Place mushrooms in a bowl, cover, and let stand for at least 4 hours. Serve hot or cold as an antipasto.

Marinated Porcini with Tomatoes and Mint

16 oz fresh porcini mushrooms, 2 cloves garlic, 2 anchovy fillets,
1 cup canned peeled tomatoes, 2 stalks mint,
⅓ cup extra-virgin olive oil, Juice of 1 lemon,
Salt, Freshly ground white pepper

Clean mushrooms with a mushroom brush or paper towel and cut into thick slices. Peel garlic and chop finely. Rinse anchovy fillets, pat dry, and cut into very thin strips. Drain tomatoes well and dice coarsely. Rinse mint and pat dry.

In a pan, heat oil then braise garlic and anchovy strips. Add mushrooms and sauté for 5 minutes. Add lemon juice and diced tomatoes. Season liberally with salt and pepper. Fold in mint, cover, and simmer over low heat for another 20 minutes. Transfer to a bowl, remove mint stalks, cover, and let stand for 2–3 hours.

This refreshing appetizer tastes best with fresh ciabatta or flatbread. This recipe can also be prepared with cremini mushrooms.

Butternut Squash with a Boletus Mushroom Filling

2 medium boletus mushrooms or 1 handful dried boletus mushrooms,
1 onion, 1 clove garlic, 1 stalk rosemary, 3 stalks cilantro,
7 sun-dried tomatoes in oil, 2 butternut squash (¾ lb each),
Extra-virgin olive oil for sautéing and brushing,
½ tsp cayenne pepper, Salt,
Freshly ground black pepper, ½ cup wild rice

Preheat oven to 425°F. Clean fresh mushrooms with a mushroom brush or paper towel, trim, and dice coarsely. Soak dried mushrooms in hot water for 5–10 minutes. Peel and dice onion and garlic. Rinse rosemary and cilantro, remove leaves from stems, and chop finely. Finely dice tomatoes. Cut squash in half lengthwise. Remove flesh and seeds from all 4 halves of the squash, making a trough about 1–1½-inches wide (there should be about ⅓ inch of flesh remaining around the edges). Finely chop squash flesh and half the seeds. Combine with onion, garlic, herbs, and tomatoes.

In a pot, heat oil then braise squash-herb mixture for 5–8 minutes. Add mushrooms and continue braising while stirring. Season with salt, pepper, and cayenne; stir in rice. Spoon mixture into squash halves and smooth out the surface. Put the halves back together and brush on all sides with oil. Wrap in aluminum foil and bake in the oven for about 75 minutes.

Bay Bolete Skewers with Turkey Breast Fillet and Two Dips

For the skewers: ²/₃ lb turkey breast fillet, 7 oz bay boletes,
1 yellow, 1 red, and 1 green bell pepper, 1 small zucchini,
1 yellow onion, Poultry seasoning
For the dips: ¹/₄ cup peanut butter,
Salt, Freshly ground white pepper, ²/₃ cup tomato ketchup,
2 tbs white wine vinegar, 1 tbs sugar, 1 tsp honey,
1 pinch ginger, 1 pinch cayenne pepper, Salt
Plus: Oil for sautéing, 10–12 skewers

For the skewers: Rinse turkey, pat dry, and dice coarsely. Clean mushrooms with a mushroom brush or paper towel and trim. Cut larger mushrooms in half or quarters. Cut bell peppers in half, remove stems, seeds and interiors, and cut into bite-sized pieces. Clean zucchini and cut into pieces the same size as the turkey. Peel onion and cut into eighths. Alternately thread pieces of turkey, mushroom, bell pepper, zucchini, and onion onto the skewers. Season with poultry seasoning. In a pan, heat oil and sauté skewers on all sides over medium heat for about 8 minutes.

For the dips: Stir together peanut butter and 3 tbs water until smooth and season with salt and pepper. To make the second dip, combine ketchup, vinegar, sugar, and honey. Season with ginger, cayenne, and salt. Serve with the skewers.

Oyster Mushrooms and Bacon

14 oz oyster mushrooms, 2 shallots, 2 oz bacon,
½ bunch Italian parsley, 3 tbs sunflower seeds, 2 tbs pine nuts,
1 tbs butter, 1 large clove garlic, Salt, Freshly ground white pepper,
2 tbs white wine, Soy sauce

Clean mushrooms with a mushroom brush or paper towel, trim, and cut into strips the width of a finger. Peel shallots. Finely dice shallots and bacon. Rinse parsley, pat dry, and remove leaves from stems. Finely chop half the leaves and set aside the other half for garnish.

Starting in a cold cast-iron pan, heat bacon and fry until crispy, while stirring. Then remove and set aside. In the same pan, without adding any fat, toast sunflower seeds and pine nuts on all sides until golden. Remove and let cool. Melt butter in the pan. Squeeze garlic through a press and braise. Add mushrooms and brown. Season with salt and pepper. After about 5 minutes, add shallots and chopped parsley. Sauté for another 5–10 minutes, while stirring. Add white wine and season with soy sauce and pepper. Fold in diced bacon, toasted sunflower seeds, and pine nuts. Serve warm on large plates. Garnish with remaining parsley.

Baked Oyster Mushrooms with Soy Sauce and Tabasco

16 oz oyster mushrooms, 4 tbs canola oil, 3 tbs white wine vinegar,
3–4 tbs soy sauce, 3 tsp tomato paste, ½ tsp herb salt,
3 drops Tabasco sauce, ½ bunch Italian parsley,
2 stalks mint, Freshly ground black pepper

Clean mushrooms with a mushroom brush or paper towel, trim, remove hard portions, and then divide coarsely.

Preheat oven to 425°F. Line a baking sheet with parchment paper and spread mushrooms on top. Combine oil, vinegar, soy sauce, tomato paste, herb salt, and Tabasco. Rinse parsley and mint, pat dry, and remove leaves from stems. Chop herbs finely and stir into sauce. Drizzle liberally onto mushrooms and bake in the oven for about 15 minutes. Grind pepper over baked mushrooms and serve.

 These baked oyster mushrooms are very popular in Spain and are often served as tapas with fresh white bread or olive flatbread.

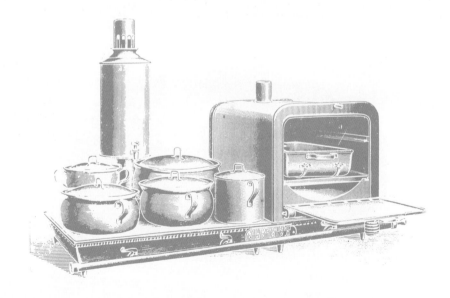

Breaded Oyster Mushrooms with Fresh Herbs

1 white onion, 4–5 cloves garlic, 1 stalk rosemary,
1 stalk thyme, 15 large basil leaves, ½ bunch chives,
15–20 medium oyster mushrooms, Salt, Freshly ground black pepper,
¼ cup extra-virgin olive oil, ¼ cup butter, 3 tsp flour,
¼ cup dry white wine, 1 cup vegetable stock, ¾ cup heavy cream,
½ tsp cumin, Juice of ½ lemon, ¼ cup Parmigiano-Reggiano,
¼ cup bread crumbs, 3 eggs, Canola oil for deep-frying

Peel onion and dice finely. Peel garlic. Using a truffle slicer or a very sharp knife, cut 2 cloves into paper-thin slices and finely dice remaining cloves. Rinse herbs and pat dry. Remove rosemary leaves from stems and chop coarsely. Strip thyme leaves from stems. Chop basil and chives finely. Clean mushrooms with a mushroom brush or paper towel, trim, and arrange on a large, deep platter. Season with salt and pepper and sprinkle with rosemary and thyme. Drizzle with olive oil and top with sliced garlic. Cover and let stand for 30 minutes.

Melt butter in a pan then braise diced onion and garlic until translucent. Dust with flour and add white wine, while stirring. Gradually add vegetable stock. Reduce sauce by about half. Stir in cream, basil, and garlic. Season with salt, pepper, cumin, and lemon juice; keep warm.

Finely grate Parmigiano-Reggiano and combine with bread crumbs in a shallow bowl. In another shallow bowl, whisk eggs thoroughly. In a large pot, heat oil for deep-frying. Dredge oyster mushrooms first in egg, then in Parmigiano-Reggiano-bread crumb mixture and fry immediately in hot oil until golden. Remove, drain on paper towels, and transfer to warm plates. Drizzle with sauce and serve immediately.

Fresh Flatbread with Honey Mushrooms in Vermouth

2 cups flour, 1½ tbs fresh yeast, 1 pinch sugar,
1 cup lukewarm water, 7 oz honey mushrooms, 1 medium onion,
1 bunch arugula, 1 small stalk rosemary, 3 tbs butter,
2 tbs Noilly Prat dry vermouth, Salt, Freshly ground pepper

Sift flour into a room-temperature bowl and make a well in the center. Completely dissolve yeast and sugar in lukewarm water and pour into the well. Gradually mix flour from the edges with the yeast mixture and process into workable dough that is not sticky. If necessary, add a little more flour. Shape dough into a ball, cover, and let rise in a warm place for 30 minutes.

In the meantime, clean mushrooms with a mushroom brush or paper towel, trim, and cut stems into small pieces. Peel onion and dice finely. Rinse arugula and rosemary and pat dry. Remove large stems from arugula and cut into wide strips. Strip rosemary leaves from stems and chop coarsely. Preheat oven to 400°F.

With your hands, shape dough into a round, flat loaf. Place on a baking sheet lined with parchment paper, and bake on the middle rack of the oven for 10 minutes. Reduce heat to 350°F and bake for another 15 minutes.

In the meantime, melt butter in a pan and braise onion. Add mushrooms and rosemary leaves. After about 5 minutes, add Noilly Prat, season with salt and pepper, and simmer for another 5 minutes. Keep mushroom mixture warm. As soon as the bread is done baking and has cooled slightly, spread mushrooms on top, sprinkle with arugula, and serve immediately.

If you love Parmiggiano-Reggiano as much as we do, shave some over the top with a vegetable peeler. A masterpiece!

Bavarian Pretzel-Dumpling Carpaccio
with Sautéed Oyster Mushrooms

For the pretzel dumpling: ½ lb day-old, unsalted soft pretzels,
½ cup milk, 1 onion, ½ bunch parsley, 1 tbs butter,
Salt, Freshly ground pepper, Freshly grated nutmeg, 3 eggs
For the salad: 1 small head iceberg lettuce, 1 small head red leaf lettuce,
21 oz oyster mushrooms, ¼ cup balsamic vinegar,
½ cup extra-virgin olive oil, Salt, Freshly ground pepper,
1 large red onion, ½ cup Parmigiano-Reggiano
Plus: Butter for the aluminum foil

For the dumpling: Cut up pretzels and place in a bowl. Heat milk and pour over the top. Peel onion and dice finely. Rinse parsley, pat dry, remove leaves, and chop. In a pan, melt butter, then braise onion until translucent. Add parsley and pour mixture over pretzels. Carefully stir in salt, pepper, nutmeg, and eggs. Shape into a thick cylinder, wrap in a sheet of buttered aluminum foil, and seal well. In a large enough pot, bring water to a boil. Place foil inside pot and simmer for about 30 minutes. Remove, unwrap foil, and let cool.

For the salad: Rinse iceberg and red leaf lettuce, spin dry, and tear into smaller pieces. Clean mushrooms with a mushroom brush or paper towel, trim, and cut up if necessary. Combine vinegar, ¼ cup oil, salt, and pepper to make a dressing. In a pan, heat remaining olive oil and brown mushrooms. Season with salt and pepper. Peel onion and cut into very thin rings. Cut pretzel dumpling into paper-thin slices and arrange on plates in a fan pattern. Arrange lettuce on the pretzels and top with onion rings and oyster mushrooms. Drizzle with dressing and shave Parmiggiano-Reggiano over the top.

Chanterelles with Tarragon and Sherry

16 oz chanterelle mushrooms, 1 onion, 1 bunch tarragon,
1–2 tbs butter, Salt, Freshly ground white pepper,
2–3 tbs dry sherry, ¼ cup heavy cream

Clean mushrooms with a mushroom brush or paper towel, trim, and cut into quarters, leaving smaller mushrooms whole. Peel and dice onion. Rinse tarragon, pat dry, and remove leaves from stems. In a pan, melt butter then brown mushrooms and onion for several minutes. Season with salt and pepper. Add tarragon and sherry. Remove pan from heat, fold in cream, and serve immediately.

If you want to use these mushrooms as an appetizer, serve them with crusty bread. They're also ideal as a side dish with meat or served lukewarm on mâche or mixed green salads.

Instead of chanterelles, use white or cremini mushrooms.

Wild Mushrooms Wrapped in Pastry
with Prosecco Sauce

For the mushrooms: 1 shallot, 1 clove garlic,
14 oz assorted wild mushrooms, 2 stalks thyme, ½ bunch parsley,
1 tbs butter, Salt, Freshly ground white pepper,
8 oz puff pastry dough (from the supermarket's refrigerated section),
1 egg yolk, 1 tbs milk
For the sauce: ⅔ cup heavy cream, ½ cup mushroom stock,
¼ cup Prosecco, 1 tsp sesame seeds, Balsamic vinegar,
Salt, Freshly ground white pepper, ¼ cup butter
Plus: Flour for the work surface

For the mushrooms: Peel shallot and garlic and dice finely. Clean mushrooms with a mushroom brush or paper towel, trim, and dice. Rinse thyme and parsley, pat dry, remove leaves from stems, and chop finely. In a pan, melt butter then braise shallot and garlic. Add mushrooms and sauté for about 2 minutes. Stir in thyme and parsley. Season with salt and pepper.

Preheat oven to 400°F. Roll out puff pastry dough on a floured surface. Spread mushroom mixture over the top and roll up the dough. Place the roll on a baking sheet lined with parchment paper and let stand. Whisk together egg yolk and milk. Brush onto the wild mushroom roll. Bake in the oven for about 25 minutes until the surface is golden.

For the sauce: In a saucepan, reduce ½ cup cream until thick and let cool. In a pot, combine stock, Prosecco, remaining cream, and sesame seeds; bring to a boil. Season with vinegar, salt, and pepper. In a saucepan, melt butter. Remove pot of sauce from heat and using a wire whisk, beat in melted butter and thickened cream.

Cut wild mushroom, roll into slices, and serve topped with sauce. Serve with a green salad or beets that have also been prepared with sesame seeds.

Instead of Prosecco, use a dry white wine.

Stir-Fried Shiitake and White Mushrooms

¾ oz dried shiitake mushrooms,
1 handful dried sengiri daikon (Asian market),
1 onion, 2 cloves garlic, 1 inch fresh ginger root,
7 oz white mushrooms, ½ Chinese cabbage,
⅔ cup frozen peas, 3–4 tbs canola oil, Soy sauce,
Salt, Freshly ground black pepper

Soak shiitakes and sengiri daikon separately in warm water for 20 minutes. Peel onion and dice finely. Peel garlic and squeeze through a press. Peel ginger and grate or chop finely. Clean white mushrooms with a mushroom brush or paper towel, trim, and slice. Clean Chinese cabbage and cut into strips. Thaw peas. Squeeze out shiitakes and daikon and cut into small pieces.

In a wok, heat oil, then braise onion, garlic, and ginger. Add shiitakes, daikon, and white mushrooms. Stir-fry for about 3 minutes. Add Chinese cabbage and peas. Stir-fry for another 2–3 minutes. Season to taste with soy sauce, salt, and pepper.

This wok dish is delicious with aromatic or jasmine rice. It's also tasty served over glass noodles as a warm Chinese salad.

Leafy Vegetables and Wood Ear Mushrooms Warm from the Pot

*1 handful dried wood ear mushrooms, ⅓ lb Swiss chard,
½ bunch arugula, 2 small endives, 2 cloves garlic,
Sunflower or canola oil for sautéing, 1 pinch herb salt,
½ tsp curry powder, Juice of ½ lemon,
Salt, Freshly ground black pepper, ¼ cup grated pecorino cheese*

Pour hot water over wood ear mushrooms and soak for 15 minutes. Clean chard. Rinse arugula, remove overly long stems, and spin dry. Clean endive, remove cores, and cut into ¾-inch pieces. Soak in lukewarm water for about 5 minutes (to remove bitter flavor) and pat dry. Peel garlic and cut into paper-thin slices with a very sharp knife. Drain mushrooms, remove hard portions, and chop coarsely.

In a tall pot, heat oil, then brown garlic slices and mushrooms on all sides. Season with herb salt and curry. Remove from pot and set aside. Add chard and endive to the hot oil and braise. Season with lemon juice, salt, and pepper. Return mushrooms and garlic to the pot and stir well. Cook until vegetables are al dente. Transfer to warm plates and scatter arugula over the top. Sprinkle with pecorino and serve immediately.

 You can vary this dish with other leafy vegetables such as Chinese cabbage, spinach, or young white cabbage. This appetizer can be eaten warm (this is how it tastes best to us), or add a few additional shots of olive oil and let it cool.

Spring Rolls with Shiitake Mushrooms

Frozen spring roll wrappers (Asian market),
4 oz fresh shiitake mushrooms,
1 small yellow and 1 small red bell pepper,
⅓ lb small peeled shrimp, ¾ inch fresh ginger root,
1 bunch cilantro, 1¾ oz glass noodles,
3 tbs peanut oil, 3 tbs oyster sauce (Asian market),
1 egg white for brushing, Oil for deep-frying,
Soy and chili sauce for dipping

Thaw spring roll wrappers on a damp paper towel. Clean shiitakes with a mushroom brush or paper towel, trim, and cut into fine strips. Cut peppers in half, remove stems, seeds, and interiors. Dice finely. Rinse shrimp, pat dry, and chop coarsely. Peel ginger and chop very finely or grate. Rinse cilantro, pat dry, remove leaves from stems, and chop coarsely. Soak noodles in hot water for 5 minutes, drain, and set aside.

In a pan, heat peanut oil and braise shiitakes, bell peppers, and shrimp. Add ginger and cilantro, stir, and season with oyster sauce. Add noodles, mix thoroughly, remove from pan, and let cool.

Arrange spring roll wrappers side by side, brush borders with egg white, and place 1 tbs filling in the center of each. Fold the sides inward, roll up the wrappers, and let stand with the seam sides down. Deep-fry rolls in hot oil in batches and serve immediately. Serve with soy sauce and chili sauce as dips.

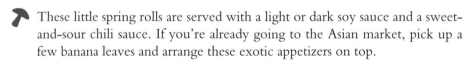 These little spring rolls are served with a light or dark soy sauce and a sweet-and-sour chili sauce. If you're already going to the Asian market, pick up a few banana leaves and arrange these exotic appetizers on top.

Vietnamese Spring Rolls with Wood Ear Mushrooms, Ground Meat, and Mint

⅓ oz dried wood ear mushrooms, 1¾ oz glass noodles,
1 bunch mint, 2 green onions, 1 large carrot,
2 oz fresh bean sprouts, ⅓ lb crabmeat,
½ lb ground meat (half beef, half pork), 1 egg,
Salt, Freshly ground black pepper,
Rice paper wrappers (Asian market),
Oil for deep-frying, Soy and chili sauce for dipping

Soak wood ear mushrooms and glass noodles separately in hot water. After 10 minutes, drain glass noodles, and using scissors, cut into pieces about ¾-inch long. After 20 minutes, drain mushrooms, pat dry, and chop finely. Rinse mint, pat dry, remove leaves from stems, and chop. Clean green onions and chop into fine rings. Clean carrot and grate finely. Thoroughly rinse bean sprouts, drain, and cut in half. Cut crabmeat into small pieces.

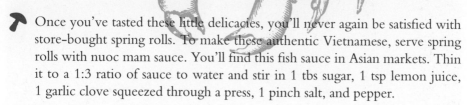

Combine ground meat, mushrooms, glass noodles, mint, green onions, carrot, bean sprouts, and crabmeat. Mix in egg. Season with salt and pepper. One at a time, spread rice paper wrappers on a kitchen towel and spray with water. Place 1–2 tbs of ground meat filling in the center. Fold the sides inward and roll up the spring roll. Cover spring rolls with a kitchen towel and let stand for about 30 minutes. Just before serving, deep-fry in batches in the hot oil. Provide soy sauce and chili sauce for dipping.

Once you've tasted these little delicacies, you'll never again be satisfied with store-bought spring rolls. To make these authentic Vietnamese, serve spring rolls with nuoc mam sauce. You'll find this fish sauce in Asian markets. Thin it to a 1:3 ratio of sauce to water and stir in 1 tbs sugar, 1 tsp lemon juice, 1 garlic clove squeezed through a press, 1 pinch salt, and pepper.

TERRINES & SOUFFLÉS

Boletus Mushroom Soufflés

*5½ oz fresh boletus mushrooms, Salt, ¼ cup butter, 2 eggs,
2 tbs béchamel sauce (prepared product from the supermarket's
refrigerated section), 1 tbs cornstarch*

Preheat oven to 400°F. Clean mushrooms with a mushroom brush or paper towel, trim, slice, and sprinkle with salt. In a pan, melt 2 tbs butter and braise mushrooms (boil away any liquid produced). Separate eggs. In a blender, purée mushrooms, egg yolks, and béchamel sauce. Beat egg whites until stiff then fold into mushroom mixture.

Generously grease 4–6 ramekins with remaining butter and dust with a little cornstarch. Fill ramekins three-quarters full with mushroom-egg mixture and place inside a large casserole dish, the bottom of which is covered with water. Bake for 20 minutes. During this time, do not open the oven door! These soufflés go well with game dishes.

Mushroom Cheese Soufflés

7 oz slippery jack or cauliflower mushrooms,
⅔ cup tangy Gouda, 1 mozzarella ball,
2 stalks marjoram, 1 small box cress, 4 eggs,
1½ tsp Dijon mustard, Salt, Freshly ground pepper,
¼ tsp freshly grated nutmeg, Butter for the ramekins

Clean slippery jack mushrooms with a mushroom brush or paper towel, trim (peel caps), and chop finely. Or, rinse cauliflower mushrooms thoroughly, pat dry, and chop finely. Grate Gouda coarsely. Dice mozzarella finely. Rinse marjoram, pat dry, remove leaves from stems, and chop coarsely. Trim cress and chop. Separate eggs and beat egg whites until stiff. Stir together egg yolks, mushrooms, Gouda, mozzarella, and mustard until smooth. Add marjoram and cress. Season with salt, pepper, and nutmeg. Carefully fold in egg whites. Spoon mixture into 4 greased ramekins and place on the middle rack of a cold oven. Set oven to 425°F and bake for 25–30 minutes. During this time, do not open the oven door!

 Generously grease the individual ramekins and fill three-quarters full. The egg whites will cause the soufflé to rise and form a golden surface. If you open the oven door before they finish baking, the soufflés will collapse. So control your curiosity and wait for the surprise—it's worth it!

Mushroom Gelatin with Ham and Broccoli Florets

1 lb broccoli, 5½ oz unblemished white mushrooms,
¼ lb cooked sliced ham, ¼ lb raw sliced ham,
Salt, 3⅓ cups canned beef stock, 2 pkgs powdered white gelatin,
¼ cup port wine, Freshly ground black pepper,
Juice of ½ lemon, Oil for the mold

Clean broccoli and separate into florets. Clean mushrooms with a mushroom brush or paper towel, trim, and cut in half. Dice ham, removing any fatty edges. Cook broccoli in boiling salted water for about 6 minutes, and then plunge into ice-water so it remains crunchy and green. Heat stock, add gelatin, and dissolve. Add port and season liberally with salt, pepper, and lemon juice. Let cool slightly.

Brush oil onto a terrine mold or loaf pan and line with plastic wrap. Pour in part of the stock, cover, and let set in the refrigerator. Top with layers of mushrooms, broccoli florets, and diced ham. Add a little more stock and set. Repeat this process until all the ingredients have been used. Cover with plastic wrap and refrigerate overnight. To serve, reverse out of the mold and slice.

Duck Liver Terrine with Wild Mushrooms and Cumberland Sauce

For the terrine: ⅓ lb duck liver paté, 1 tbs Madeira,
1 tbs port wine, 1 handful walnuts, 1 tsp dried thyme,
5½ oz assorted wild mushrooms (e.g., field, horn of plenty, boletus),
Several stalks parsley, 3½ oz barding fat (shaved), 1 tbs butter
For the cumberland sauce: 2 tbs orange juice, 2–3 tbs port wine,
¼ cup currant jelly, 1 tsp Dijon mustard,
Salt, Freshly ground black pepper, 1 tsp Worcestershire sauce

For the terrine: On the day before, combine duck liver paté, Madeira, and port in a bowl. Stir until smooth. Chop walnuts. Add walnuts and thyme to the mixture, cover, and refrigerate. Clean mushrooms with a mushroom brush or paper towel, trim, and cut into pieces. Rinse parsley, pat dry, remove leaves from stems, and chop finely. Remove rind from barding fat. In a pan, heat butter and brown mushrooms for 2–3 minutes. When just about done, add parsley. Drain mushroom mixture in a colander and let cool. On a stack of 2–3 sheets of aluminum foil about 11-inches long, arrange barding fat slices so they overlap slightly, leaving about 1 inch of foil uncovered on either side. Stir mushrooms into the duck liver mixture and place in the center of the barding fat slices. Carefully fold the sides of the fat inward, placing additional slices on top if necessary to cover the paté. When the paté is completely covered by fat, roll up tightly in aluminum foil and refrigerate overnight.

On the following day, make the cumberland sauce: In a small saucepan, heat orange juice, port, jelly, and mustard. Stir until smooth. Season with salt, pepper, and Worcestershire sauce. Bring to a boil while stirring and reduce slightly. Let cool, and just before serving, stir well.

Before serving the terrine, unwrap it and slice it with a sharp knife. Arrange on plates with 1 tbs cumberland sauce. Serve with a fresh baguette.

This terrine can be prepared in advance and is ideal as a small appetizer. It's easier to make than a terrine that uses fresh duck liver.

Venison and Boletus Mushroom Paté

1 lb venison loin, 3 stalks fresh oregano, 2 large boletus mushrooms,
2 small cloves garlic, 1 green onion, ¾ cup heavy cream,
¼ cup butter, Salt, Freshly ground white pepper, 1 pinch ground allspice,
½ tsp cinnamon, 6 leaves white gelatin, ¼ cup Madeira,
½ lb butter, Oil for the mold, 1 handful pink peppercorns

Rinse venison, pat dry, and dice coarsely. Rinse oregano, pat dry, and strip leaves from stems. Clean mushrooms with a mushroom brush or paper towel, trim, and cut into strips. Peel garlic and dice finely. Clean green onion and chop into fine rings. Whip cream until stiff and refrigerate.

In a pan, heat 2 tbs butter then brown venison on all sides over medium heat. Add oregano and garlic. Season with salt, pepper, allspice, and cinnamon. Remove meat and let cool. Melt remaining butter in the pan and braise onion rings until translucent. Add mushrooms and braise for about 5 minutes. Season with salt and pepper. Remove from pan.

Soak gelatin according to directions. In a small saucepan, heat Madeira and dissolve gelatin. In another saucepan, melt butter and let cool.

Purée venison in a blender while gradually adding port, gelatin, and butter. Using a wire whisk, fold in cream. Season to taste with salt and pepper. Let cool.

Brush oil onto a terrine mold or loaf pan and line with plastic wrap. Spoon in part of the meat mixture, cover, and refrigerate for 30 minutes. Continue adding alternating layers of mushrooms, pink peppercorns, and meat, covering and refrigerating after each meat layer, until all the ingredients have been used. Cover with plastic wrap and refrigerate overnight.

Chicken Paté with Boletus Mushrooms and Cranberries

2 small cloves garlic, 3 stalks fresh thyme, 2 large boletus mushrooms,
¾ cup heavy cream, ½ cup fresh cranberries, 1 lb chicken liver,
3–4 tbs extra-virgin olive oil, Salt, Freshly ground white pepper,
2 tbs butter, 4 leaves white gelatin, ¼ cup port wine,
1 cup butter, Oil for the mold, 1 tbs pink peppercorns

Peel garlic and dice finely. Rinse thyme, pat dry, and strip leaves from stems. Clean mushrooms with a mushroom brush or paper towel, trim, and dice. Whip cream until stiff and refrigerate. Rinse cranberries, drain, and clean. Rinse chicken liver and pat dry.

In a pan, heat oil and brown liver on all sides over medium heat. Add garlic and thyme. Season with salt and pepper. Remove from heat and let cool. In another pan, heat butter then brown mushrooms for about 5 minutes. Season with salt and pepper. Soak gelatin according to directions. In a small saucepan, heat port. Squeeze out gelatin and dissolve in the port. In a small saucepan, melt butter and let cool slightly.

In a blender, purée liver while gradually pouring in the port-gelatin mixture and melted butter. Put the mixture through a fine strainer, fold in cream, season to taste with salt and pepper, and let cool.

Brush oil onto a terrine mold or loaf pan and line with plastic wrap. Pour in part of the liver mixture and top with layers of mushrooms, pink peppercorns, and cranberries. Repeat this process until all the ingredients have been used. Cover with plastic wrap and refrigerate overnight.

On the following day, reverse onto a platter and cut into slices about ½-inch thick (preferably with an electric knife).

Arrange the terrine on mâche or frisée lettuce and serve with a baguette.

Beef Terrine with Mushrooms and Pink Peppercorns

1 lb calf's liver, ¼ cup butter,
Salt, Freshly ground white pepper,
7 oz cremini mushrooms,
2 small cloves garlic,
¾ cup heavy cream,
6 leaves white gelatin,
½ cup port wine, 1 cup butter,
2–3 tsp pink peppercorns,
Oil for the mold

Rinse calf's liver, pat dry, and dice coarsely. In a pan, heat 3 tsp butter, then brown liver on all sides over medium heat. Remove from the pan and let cool. Season with salt and pepper. Clean mushrooms with a mushroom brush or paper towel, trim, and cut into quarters. Peel garlic and mince. Whip cream until stiff, cover, and refrigerate for about 15 minutes. Soak gelatin according to package directions.

Heat remaining butter in the pan and braise mushrooms and garlic. Add half the port and let cool. In a small saucepan, melt butter. Add remaining port. Squeeze out gelatin and add. Heat until the gelatin has completely dissolved. In a blender, purée liver while gradually pouring in melted butter. Add port-gelatin mixture and season with salt and pepper. Gently fold in cream.

Pour one-third of the liver mixture into a greased terrine mold or loaf pan lined with plastic wrap and smooth out the surface. Top with a layer of mushrooms and a layer of pink peppercorns. Repeat this process until all the ingredients have been used. Cover with plastic wrap and refrigerate for at least 6–8 hours. Reverse terrine onto a platter and cut into ½-inch slices.

Serve this delicious and elegant terrine with a crispy baguette and fresh green salad.

RICE & PASTA DISHES

Porcini Risotto with Prosecco

1 onion, 1 clove garlic, 3 medium porcini mushrooms,
½ bunch Italian parsley, ¼ cup Parmigiano-Reggiano,
4 cups hearty beef stock, ¼ cup extra-virgin olive oil,
1⅓ cups Arborio rice, 2 tbs butter, Salt,
Freshly ground black pepper, ½ cup Prosecco

Peel onion and garlic and dice finely. Clean mushrooms with a mushroom brush or paper towel and trim. Slice the caps and dice the stems. Rinse parsley, pat dry, remove leaves from stems, and chop coarsely. Using a vegetable peeler, shave part of the Parmigiano-Reggiano and finely grate the rest. In a saucepan, heat stock. In a large saucepan, heat olive oil and sweat onion and garlic. Add rice and braise for about 3 minutes until translucent. Add just enough stock to cover the rice and reduce slightly. Simmer for 15–20 minutes while stirring constantly, adding enough stock so the rice is barely covered. In a pan, melt butter and brown mushrooms on all sides. Season with salt and pepper. Five minutes before the risotto is done, stir in mushrooms, Prosecco, and grated Parmigiano-Reggiano. Transfer to large, warm plates. Sprinkle with shaved Parmigiano-Reggiano and garnish with parsley. Serve immediately.

Risotto with Chanterelles

2 small onions, 1 clove garlic, 16 oz chanterelle mushrooms,
About 2½ cups chicken stock, 3 tbs butter, 1 cup Arborio rice,
Several saffron threads, 1 tsp dried thyme, ½ cup white wine,
Salt, Freshly ground white pepper, ¼ cup cold butter,
2 heaping tbs freshly grated Parmigiano-Reggiano

Peel onions and garlic and dice finely. Clean mushrooms with a mushroom brush or paper towel, trim, and cut large mushrooms into smaller pieces. In a saucepan, heat stock. In a large pan, melt half the butter and sweat half the onions and garlic. Add rice and braise for 2 minutes until translucent. Crush saffron threads in a mortar. Add saffron and thyme to the rice. Add just enough stock to cover the rice. Simmer while stirring constantly until all the liquid has been absorbed. Add more stock and, finally, the wine. Continue stirring and simmer for a total of 15–20 minutes until all the liquid is gone. Heat remaining butter in a pan, then sweat remaining onions and garlic. Add mushrooms and sauté for about 4 minutes. Season with salt and pepper. Cut butter into pieces and stir cold pieces of butter and Parmigiano-Reggiano into the risotto. Stir in mushrooms and serve immediately.

Enrich the risotto by folding in a little semi-stiff cream. Garnish it with fresh thyme stalks or parsley. Serve as an entrée or as a side with meat dishes.

Penne with Porcini Sauce

1 oz dried porcini mushrooms, 2 small onions,
1 clove garlic, 1 lb penne pasta, Salt, 2 tbs butter,
¼ cup Noilly Prat dry vermouth, ⅔ cup heavy cream,
Freshly ground pepper, ¼ cup Parmigiano-Reggiano

Soak mushrooms in hot water for about 30 minutes. Peel onions and dice finely. Peel garlic and squeeze through a press. Drain mushrooms, setting aside about ½ cup of the soaking water. Boil pasta in a large amount of salted water according to package directions until al dente. In a pan, melt butter, then brown onions and garlic. Add mushrooms and sauté for about 3 minutes. Add mushroom water and vermouth; reduce slightly. Add cream and bring to a boil. Season liberally with salt and pepper. Grate Parmigiano-Reggiano. Pour sauce on top of the penne and sprinkle with cheese. Serve immediately.

Papardelle with Assorted Wild Mushrooms

14 oz assorted mushrooms (e.g., horn of plenty, bay bolete, chanterelle, oyster, field, white, cremini), 2 small cloves garlic, ½ bunch Italian parsley, 2 tbs Parmigiano-Reggiano, 3 tbs extra-virgin olive oil, Salt, Freshly ground black pepper, 1 pinch chili powder, Juice of ½ lemon, 1 lb papardelle pasta

Clean mushrooms with a mushroom brush or paper towel, trim, and cut in half. Remove any hard portions from oyster mushrooms. Peel garlic and mince. Rinse parsley, pat dry, remove leaves from stems, and chop finely. Using a vegetable peeler, thinly shave Parmigiano-Reggiano. In a pan, heat olive oil, then brown mushrooms. Add garlic and braise. Season with salt, pepper, and chili powder. Sauté mushrooms for about 5 minutes. Remove from the pan, drizzle with lemon juice, and keep warm. Boil pasta in salted water according to package directions until al dente, drain, and transfer to a warm bowl. Add mushrooms, sprinkle with part of the parsley, all of the Parmigiano-Reggiano, and stir. Arrange on warm plates, sprinkle with remaining parsley, grind pepper over the top, and serve immediately.

Spaghetti with White Mushrooms and Shrimp

2 shallots, 10½ oz white mushrooms, 2 cloves garlic,
2 tomatoes, 1 lb spaghetti, Salt, 2 tbs butter, ½ cup white wine,
¾ cup heavy cream, ⅔ lb peeled shrimp,
Freshly ground white pepper, 1 tbs dry Italian herb mixture

Peel and dice shallots. Clean mushrooms with a mushroom brush or paper towel, trim, and slice. Peel garlic and squeeze through a press. Cut an X through the skin of the tomatoes, blanch in boiling water, peel, remove seeds and cores, and dice finely.

Boil spaghetti in a large amount of salted water according to package directions until al dente. In a pan, melt butter, then brown shallots and mushrooms for about 3 minutes while stirring. Add garlic and braise. Add wine, cream, shrimp, and diced tomatoes. Simmer for 6–8 minutes. Season with salt, pepper, and Italian herbs. Serve sauce with spaghetti.

Spaghetti in Morel Sauce with Chicken

5½ oz fresh morels (or ½ oz dried), ½ lb chicken breast fillet,
Salt, 1 onion, 1 stalk celery, 1 lb spaghetti, 3 tbs butter,
⅔ cup white wine, ¾ cup heavy cream,
Freshly ground black pepper, 2 tbs grated Parmigiano-Reggiano

Rinse morels and trim (soak dried mushrooms in hot water for 30 minutes, then rinse, and pat dry), cutting into smaller pieces if necessary. Rinse chicken breast, pat dry, cut into strips, and salt. Peel onion and dice. Clean celery and cut into thin slices.

Boil spaghetti in a large amount of salted water according to package directions until al dente. Melt half the butter in a pan. Sauté chicken on all sides, remove from pan, and set aside. Melt remaining butter, then sweat onion and celery. Add morels and brown. Add white wine and cream, season with salt, and pepper. Simmer for 5 minutes. Return chicken to the pan and heat. Drain pasta, transfer to a bowl, and toss with the sauce. Serve with grated Parmigiano-Reggiano.

Quick Stir-Fried Tagliatelle

4½ oz oyster mushrooms, 4½ oz white mushrooms,
2 oz fresh shiitake mushrooms, 1 onion, 1 clove garlic,
1 lb tagliatelle, Salt, ¼ cup peanut oil, 1–2 tbs soy sauce,
1 pinch coriander, 1 tbs chopped cilantro

Clean mushrooms with a mushroom brush or paper towel, trim, and cut into small pieces. Peel onion and garlic and dice finely. Boil tagliatelle in a large amount of salted water according to package directions until al dente.

In a wok, heat peanut oil, add mushrooms, and stir-fry for about 3 minutes. Add onion and garlic and stir-fry for about 2 minutes. Add soy sauce, reduce heat immediately, and season with salt and coriander. Add pasta and toss with mushrooms. Sprinkle with cilantro and serve.

Macaroni Casserole with White Mushrooms

Salt, ⅓ lb macaroni, 1 onion, 1 clove garlic,
16 oz white mushrooms, ½ bunch parsley, ⅓ cup Gruyère,
2 tbs butter, Freshly ground white pepper
For the béchamel sauce: 3 tbs butter, 3 tbs flour, 1¾ cups milk,
Salt, Freshly ground white pepper, 1 pinch freshly grated nutmeg,
1 tsp lemon juice, ¼ cup crème fraîche
Plus: Butter for the casserole dish

Bring a large amount of salted water to a boil, cook macaroni according to package directions until al dente, drain, and keep warm. Peel onion and garlic and dice finely. Clean mushrooms with a mushroom brush or paper towel, trim, and slice. Rinse parsley, pat dry, remove leaves from stems, and chop finely. Grate Gruyère.

In a pan, melt butter and braise onion and garlic until translucent. Add mushrooms and brown on all sides. Season with salt and pepper and sprinkle with parsley.

Preheat oven to 350°F. For the béchamel sauce: In a saucepan, melt butter and stir in flour. Add milk while stirring constantly. Make a roux and simmer over low heat for 15 minutes, stirring occasionally. Season with salt, pepper, nutmeg, and lemon juice.

Line a buttered casserole dish with some of the macaroni. Sprinkle about one-third of the cheese, top with 2–3 tbs mushrooms, spoon on a little crème fraîche, and pour on one-third of the béchamel sauce. Repeat this process 2 more times until all the ingredients have been used. Finish with a layer of cheese. Bake in the oven for about 30 minutes until golden.

Cannelloni with Fresh Chanterelles and Spinach

2 cloves garlic, 2 small green onions,
9 oz chanterelle mushrooms, 1 lb spinach,
Salt, 3 tbs butter, Freshly ground black pepper,
½ cup heavy cream, ⅔ cup ricotta cheese, 3 eggs,
½ cup grated Emmenthaler, 2 tbs bread crumbs,
15–20 lasagna noodles, 1 mozzarella ball

Peel garlic and mince. Clean green onions and chop into fine rings. Clean mushrooms with a mushroom brush or paper towel, trim, and cut larger mushrooms in half or into quarters. Clean spinach thoroughly, rinse, and drain. In a tall pot, melt 1 tbs butter, braise spinach over medium heat for about 4 minutes, and season with salt. Remove spinach with a slotted spoon, squeeze out thoroughly, and chop coarsely. Melt another 1 tbs of butter and sweat garlic and green onions. Add mushrooms, season with salt and pepper, and brown. Return spinach to the pot, add cream and reduce for about 5 minutes. Transfer pot contents to a large bowl, cover and let cool. Combine ricotta, eggs, Emmenthaler, and bread crumbs until smooth. Combine with the cooled spinach-mushroom mixture.

Preheat oven to 350°F. Cook lasagna noodles in salted water until al dente, drain, and arrange side by side. Place 3 tbs of the spinach filling on each noodle and roll up starting from one of the long sides. Place cannelloni in a buttered casserole dish with the seam-side down. Bake in the oven for about 25 minutes. Cut mozzarella into thin slices. About 5–10 minutes before the cannelloni are done, top with cheese and bake until golden-brown.

Porcini Ravioli with Sage Butter

For the dough: 1⅓ cups flour, 2 eggs,
¼–½ cup lukewarm water, ½ tsp salt, 1 tbs olive oil
For the filling: 2 medium porcini mushrooms,
1 green onion, 1 clove garlic, 2 tbs Parmigiano-Reggiano, 2 tbs butter,
Salt, Freshly ground black pepper, ⅔ cup ricotta cheese, 1 egg, 1–2 tbs bread crumbs
Plus: Flour for the work surface, 1 egg white for brushing,
10–12 fresh sage leaves, ¼ cup butter

For the dough: Sift flour into a bowl and make a well in the center. Place eggs, water, salt, and oil in the well. Process these ingredients into a workable dough. Shape into a ball, wrap in plastic wrap, and refrigerate for about 20 minutes.

For the filling: Clean mushrooms with a mushroom brush or paper towel, trim, and cut into narrow strips. Clean green onion, peel garlic, and finely dice both. Grate Parmigiano-Reggiano.

In a pan, melt butter, then braise green onion and garlic until translucent. Add mushrooms and brown on all sides. Season with salt and pepper. Remove from the pan and let cool. Stir ricotta until creamy and fold in mushrooms. Add egg, bread crumbs, and Parmigiano-Reggiano; mix well. Season to taste with salt and pepper.

On a floured surface, roll out pasta dough into a thin sheet and cut out circles with a 2- to 3-inch diameter. Place 1 tsp filling in the center of each circle and brush borders with egg white. Fold over into semicircles and press edges together lightly with the tines of a fork. Continue making ravioli until all the dough and mushroom filling has been used. Let ravioli dry on a floured surface for about 10 minutes.

Cook ravioli in boiling salted water for 5 minutes and remove with a slotted spoon. Rinse sage leaves and pat dry. In a pan, melt butter and stir in sage leaves. Transfer ravioli to warm plates, pour sage butter over the top, and serve.

Spinach Ravioli with White Truffles

For the dough: 1 cup flour, 2 eggs, 1 egg yolk, ½ tsp salt
For the filling: 1 clove garlic, 1 small green onion,
1¼–1⅓ lb spinach, ¼ cup butter, ¼ cup heavy cream,
Salt, Freshly ground white pepper, Freshly grated nutmeg
Plus: Flour for the work surface, Egg white for brushing,
¼ cup freshly grated Parmigiano-Reggiano, 3 tbs white truffles

For the dough: Sift flour into a bowl and make a well in the center. Place eggs, egg yolk, and salt in the well. Quickly process all these ingredients into a workable dough. If the dough is too firm, add 1–2 tbs lukewarm water. Shape dough into a ball, wrap in plastic wrap, and refrigerate for about 20 minutes.

For the filling: Peel garlic, clean green onion, and slice both finely. Rinse spinach thoroughly, clean, and spin dry. In a large pot, melt butter, and braise garlic and green onion until translucent. Gradually add spinach and let wilt. Add cream and continue braising until the liquid has almost evaporated. Season with salt, pepper, and nutmeg. Set aside and let cool.

Roll out dough on a floured surface to the thickness of the back of a knife blade and cut out circles with a 2- to 3-inch diameter. Place 1 tsp spinach filling in the center of each circle and brush borders with egg white. Fold over into semicircles and press edges together lightly with the tines of a fork. Continue making ravioli until all the dough and spinach filling has been used. Let ravioli dry on a floured surface for about 10 minutes.

Cook in boiling salted water for 5 minutes and remove with a slotted spoon. Transfer finished ravioli to warm plates, sprinkle with Parmigiano-Reggiano, and slice truffles over the top. Serve immediately.

Pumpkin Gnocchi with White Truffles

1½ lb pumpkin, 1 lb all-purpose potatoes, Salt,
2 eggs, ½ cup durum wheat semolina, ¼ cup cornstarch
¼ cup butter, Freshly ground black pepper, Freshly grated nutmeg,
1¾ oz white truffles, Flour for the work surface

Preheat oven to 400°F. Cut pumpkin into pieces the width of a finger, wrap in aluminum foil, and bake in the oven for 60 minutes. Remove foil, place pumpkin in a bowl, and let cool. Peel potatoes, rinse, and boil in salted water for 20 minutes until done. Pour off water, put warm potatoes through a ricer, and add to pumpkins. Mix potatoes, pumpkin, eggs, semolina, cornstarch, and 1 pinch salt into a dough. On a floured work surface, shape dough into a cylinder the thickness of a finger. Using a knife cut into 1-inch pieces and press a pattern into the top of each piece with the tines of a fork. Bring a large amount of salted water to a boil and simmer gnocchi for 4 minutes. Remove with a slotted spoon. In a pan, melt butter and sauté gnocchi until golden. Season to taste with salt, pepper, and nutmeg. Transfer to warm plates and slice white truffles over the top.

Gnocchi with Cremini Mushrooms and Gorgonzola

1 lb gnocchi (from the supermarket's refrigerated section),
Salt, 14 oz cremini mushrooms, 1 onion, ½ bunch parsley,
1 tbs butter, ⅔ cup Gorgonzola, ¾ cup heavy cream,
½ cup milk, Freshly ground white pepper, 1 handful walnuts

Boil gnocchi in a large amount of salted water according to package directions, drain, and keep warm. Clean mushrooms with a mushroom brush or paper towel, trim, and cut into small pieces. Peel onion and dice finely. Rinse parsley, pat dry, remove leaves from stems, and chop. In a large pan, melt butter, then brown mushrooms and onion for 3 minutes. Cut up Gorgonzola, add to mushrooms, and melt. Add cream and milk, and reduce. Season with salt and pepper. Stir in walnuts. Transfer gnocchi to a warm bowl, toss with the sauce, and sprinkle with chopped parsley.

Bavarian Potato Noodles with Shiitakes and Turnips

For the noodles: ⅓ lb all-purpose potatoes,
1 cup flour, 1 egg yolk, Salt
For the mushrooms and turnip mixture:
8–10 medium fresh shiitake mushrooms,
3 turnips, 1 white onion, 3 tbs butter,
Salt, Freshly ground pepper, Freshly grated nutmeg,
½ cup lukewarm water, 2 tbs olive oil
Plus: Flour for the work surface, Fine semolina for dredging

For the potato noodles: Boil potatoes until done, peel, and put through a ricer while warm. Combine potatoes and flour. Add egg yolk and salt. Gradually add 2–3 tbs cold water and mix into a firm dough. Shape dough into a ball, wrap in plastic wrap, and refrigerate for 20–30 minutes.

Clean shiitakes with a mushroom brush or paper towel, trim, and slice. Peel turnips and onion and dice. In a pan, heat butter and braise turnips and onion. Add salt and pepper and season to taste with nutmeg. Add water, cover, and simmer over medium heat for 5 minutes until al dente. Remove vegetables from pan and keep warm. Heat oil in the pan, brown shiitakes on all sides, and season lightly with salt and pepper. Remove from heat and let stand.

Bring a large amount of salted water to a boil. Pinch off hazelnut-sized pieces of dough and using your hands, roll into noodles on a floured work surface. Dredge noodles in fine semolina. Continue the process until all the dough has been used. Place noodles in simmering water for 5 minutes, remove with a slotted spoon, and add to turnip mixture. Mix well and arrange on warm plates. Spread sautéed shiitakes over the top and serve immediately.

HEARTY ENTRÉES

Black Forest Poacher's Pan

2½ oz bacon, 25–28 oz assorted mushrooms (e.g., chanterelle, boletus, bay bolete),
½ bunch parsley, 2 tbs butter, Salt, Freshly ground black pepper,
⅔ cup heavy cream, 1 egg

Dice bacon finely. Clean mushrooms with a mushroom brush or paper towel, trim, and slice. Rinse parsley, pat dry, remove leaves from stems, and chop finely. In a large pan, melt butter and brown bacon. Add mushrooms and braise for about 10 minutes. Season with salt and pepper. Whisk together cream and egg, stir into mushrooms, and let set. Serve garnished with parsley.

Serve poacher's pan with dumplings or a plain baguette.

Mushroom Ragout

*1 onion, 25 oz assorted fresh mushrooms, 1 bunch parsley,
2 tbs butter, 2 tbs paprika, Salt, Freshly ground black pepper,
2 tbs tomato paste, 2 cups instant mushroom stock,
½ cup Noilly Prat dry vermouth, 1 cup heavy cream,
Juice of ½ lemon, Garlic salt*

Peel and dice onion. Clean mushrooms with a mushroom brush or paper towel, trim, and cut into pieces. Rinse parsley, pat dry, remove leaves from stems, and chop finely. In a large pan, melt butter and braise onion. Add mushrooms, brown and season with paprika, salt, and pepper. Stir in tomato paste and sauté for another 3 minutes. Add stock and vermouth. Reduce over medium heat for 8–10 minutes. When almost done, add cream and lemon juice. Season to taste with garlic salt. Just before serving, sprinkle with chopped parsley.

Serve with Bavarian pretzel-dumpling (recipe on page 47).

If you don't have dry vermouth on hand, use white wine instead.

Fried Potatoes with Favorite
Mushrooms and Chives

*⅔ lb bacon, 17 oz of your favorite mushrooms (fantastic with
cauliflower mushrooms!), 1 small green onion, ¾ lb cooked, firm potatoes,
1 bunch chives, Salt, Freshly ground pepper, 2 tbs butter*

Dice bacon, removing gristle and rind. Clean mushrooms with a mushroom brush or paper towel, trim, and cut into thin slices. Clean green onion and chop into fine rings. Slice cooled potatoes. Rinse chives, pat dry, and chop into rolls. In a cast-iron pan, render bacon and fry until crispy. Add green onion and braise. Add mushrooms immediately and sauté for 5 minutes. Season with salt and pepper. Remove mushroom mixture from pan and keep warm. Melt butter in the pan then sauté potatoes until golden-brown. Season with salt and pepper. Arrange fried potatoes on warm plates. Top with mushrooms and garnish liberally with chives.

Mushroom Potato Gratin

1 onion, 2 cloves garlic, 12 oz cremini mushrooms, 1⅓ lb firm potatoes,
½ cup Gruyère or Emmenthaler, ¾ cup heavy cream,
½ cup milk, Salt, Freshly ground pepper, ½ tsp ground sesame,
½ tsp sweet paprika, 2 tbs butter, Butter for the casserole dish

Preheat oven to 350°F. Peel onion and garlic and dice finely. Clean mushrooms with a mushroom brush or paper towel, trim, and cut into thin slices. Peel potatoes, rinse, and cut into thin slices. Grate cheese coarsely. Whisk cream and milk together and season with salt, pepper, sesame, and paprika. In a pan, melt 2 tbs butter and braise onion and garlic until translucent. Add mushrooms and sauté for 5 minutes. Season with salt and pepper. In a buttered casserole dish, arrange half the potato slices in a fan pattern. Spread part of the mushrooms on top of the potatoes and sprinkle with cheese. Top with layers of the remaining potatoes, mushrooms, and again sprinkle with cheese. Add cream mixture. Bake in the oven on the middle rack for 1 hour until golden.

Asian Mushroom Stir-Fry

*3½ oz dried shiitake mushrooms, Several dried wood ear mushrooms,
2 leeks, 2 red chile peppers, 2 cloves garlic, 10½ oz cremini mushrooms,
2 tomatoes, 2 tbs coriander seeds, 1 dried chile pepper,
¼ cup peanut oil, 1 tsp cumin, ½ cup plain yogurt,
1 tsp turmeric, Salt, Cilantro*

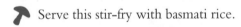

Soak shiitake and wood ear mushrooms in hot water for 30 minutes. Clean leeks, rinse well, and cut into thin rings. Cut bell peppers in half, remove stems, seeds and interiors, and dice. Peel garlic and dice finely. Clean cremini mushrooms with a mushroom brush or paper towel, trim, and cut in half. Cut an X through the skin of the tomatoes, blanch, peel, remove cores, and dice. Crush coriander seeds and dried chile pepper separately in a mortar. Drain mushrooms and cut into strips, setting aside ½ cup of the soaking water.

In a wok or large pan, heat oil and roast coriander and cumin. Add and stir-fry leeks, bell peppers, and garlic for about 2 minutes. Add all mushrooms, diced tomatoes, and ½ cup water. Continue simmering for another 3 minutes. Add yogurt and simmer for another 3 minutes, stirring constantly. Season with chile pepper, turmeric, and salt until reduced, about 8 minutes. Serve garnished with cilantro.

Serve this stir-fry with basmati rice.

Wontons with Shiitakes and Cilantro

2 all-purpose potatoes, Salt, 5 oz fresh shiitake mushrooms,
1 small onion, 3 tbs peanut oil, Freshly ground white pepper,
1 tsp coriander, 1 pinch ginger, 1 bunch cilantro,
1 tsp sesame oil, About 20 frozen wonton skins, 1 egg white

Boil potatoes in salted water until done, peel, put through a ricer, and transfer to a bowl. Clean shiitakes with a mushroom brush or paper towel, trim, and dice finely. Peel onion and mince. In a pan, heat peanut oil and brown mushrooms and onions. Season with salt, pepper, coriander, and ginger. Rinse cilantro, pat dry, remove leaves from stems, and chop finely. Add mushrooms and cilantro to potatoes and stir. Flavor with sesame oil.

Thaw wonton skins under a damp kitchen towel. Place a little of the mushroom mixture on each one. Brush borders with egg white and close the skins around the filling to form small pockets. Cook wontons in gently simmering, salted water for about 2 minutes. Remove and arrange on a warm platter.

Serve wontons on a bed of vegetables, such as snow peas, and drizzle with soy sauce.

Bavarian Bread Dumplings
with Cream Mushrooms

For the dumplings: 1½ cups milk, 10 stale rolls,
3 tsp salt, ½ bunch parsley, 1 onion, 3 eggs
For the mushrooms: 35 oz assorted wild mushrooms,
1 small onion, 1 tbs butter, 1 tbs flour, ½ cup heavy cream,
Salt, Freshly ground white pepper, Juice of ½ lemon
Plus: Chopped parsley

For the dumplings: Heat milk. Cut rolls into thin slices and toss in a bowl with 2 tsp salt. Pour hot milk over the top, cover, and let stand for about 15 minutes. Rinse parsley, pat dry, remove leaves from stems, and chop finely. Peel onion and chop. Add parsley, onion and eggs to rolls, and knead into a smooth dough. In a large pot, bring salted water to a boil. With moistened hands, shape dough into 8 dumplings and place in boiling water. Simmer over low heat for about 20 minutes.

For the mushrooms: Clean wild mushrooms with a mushroom brush or paper towel, trim, and cut into fine slices. Peel onion and chop finely. In a large pan, heat butter and braise onion until translucent. Add mushrooms and sauté for 2–3 minutes, while stirring constantly. Dust with flour, stir well, and continue cooking over low heat for about 5 minutes. Add cream and bring to a boil. Season to taste with salt, pepper, and lemon juice.

When done, remove dumplings from the pot with a slotted spoon and arrange on warm plates with the mushrooms. Garnish with chopped parsley.

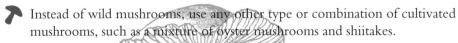 Instead of wild mushrooms, use any other type or combination of cultivated mushrooms, such as a mixture of oyster mushrooms and shiitakes.

Bread Dumplings with Boletus Sauce

For the dumplings: 1 oz dried boletus mushrooms,
¼ cup dry sherry, 1½ cups milk, 1¾ cups stale rolls,
Salt, 1 medium onion, A little butter, 2 eggs
For the sauce: 1 onion, ¼ lb diced bacon, 1 tbs Dijon mustard,
¾ cup vegetable stock, 1 bunch parsley, ⅔ cup ricotta cheese,
Salt, Freshly ground pepper, Juice of ½ lemon

For the dumplings: Soak mushrooms in sherry for 30 minutes. Heat milk. Cut rolls into pieces, place in a bowl, add milk, and season with salt. Cover and soak for about 20 minutes. Peel onion and dice. In a pan, melt butter, then braise onion. Add onion to rolls. Squeeze out mushrooms, chop finely, and add to rolls. Set aside the sherry. Add eggs and knead mixture thoroughly. With moistened hands, shape the mixture into dumplings. In a large pot, bring salted water to a boil, add dumplings, and simmer over medium heat for 15–20 minutes until done.

For the sauce: Peel onion and dice finely. In an ungreased nonstick pan, render bacon. Add onion and braise until translucent. Stir in mustard. Add sherry and stock; bring to a boil. Rinse parsley, pat dry, remove leaves from stems, and chop finely. Add ricotta and two-thirds of the parsley; heat (do not return to a boil). Season liberally with salt, pepper, and lemon juice. Remove dumplings from the pot, arrange on warm plates with the mushroom sauce and garnish with parsley.

"Försterin-Style" Pancakes

For the batter: 1 cup flour, 1 tsp salt, 1½ cups milk, 2 eggs
For the filling: 14 oz assorted mushrooms, 2 shallots,
1 clove garlic, ½ bunch parsley, ¼ cup oil, Salt,
Freshly ground black pepper, Freshly grated nutmeg,
½ cup grated Swiss cheese, ⅔ cup sour cream
Plus: Butter for frying the pancakes

For the batter: In a bowl, combine flour, salt, and milk. Add eggs and stir well. Let stand for 30 minutes. If the batter is too thick, stir in a little more milk.

For the filling: Clean mushrooms with a mushroom brush or paper towel, trim, and dice. Peel shallots and garlic and dice finely. Rinse parsley, pat dry, remove leaves from stems, and chop. In a pan, heat oil, then brown mushrooms. Add shallots and garlic and braise for 2 minutes. Season liberally with salt, pepper, and nutmeg. Stir in cheese and sour cream. Add parsley and bring to a boil.

In a large pan, heat butter and make 4 pancakes, one at a time (keep first pancakes warm while the others are cooking). Top each pancake with mushroom filling, roll up, and serve immediately.

Pancake Tower with Mushrooms, Herbs, Almonds, and Ricotta

For the batter: 1 cup flour, 3 eggs, 1¼ cups milk, 1 pinch salt
For the filling: 7 oz cremini mushrooms, ½ bunch arugula,
½ bunch sorrel, 2 apples (preferably Jonagold), 1 cup ricotta cheese,
1 cup sour cream, ½ cup ground almonds,
Freshly ground black pepper, ½ cup grated Emmenthaler
Plus: Butter for frying and casserole dish

For the batter: Combine flour, eggs, milk, and salt. Cover and let stand for 20 minutes.

For the filling: Clean mushrooms with a mushroom brush or paper towel, trim, and slice. Rinse arugula and sorrel, pat dry, remove hard stems, and chop coarsely. Peel apples, cut into quarters, remove cores, and grate coarsely. Combine ricotta, sour cream, almonds, and grated apples. Season with pepper.

Preheat oven to 325°F. In a small pan, heat butter and make 6 small pancakes. Keep warm in the oven. When all the dough is used, spread the first pancake with the ricotta mixture, top with mushrooms and part of the herbs, and sprinkle with grated Emmenthaler. Top the second pancake in the same way and place it on top of the first. Continue this process until all 6 pancakes are stacked on top of one another and all the filling ingredients have been used. Place stack in a greased casserole dish and bake in the oven on the middle rack for 20 minutes.

English Casserole with Oyster Mushrooms and Curry Sauce

16 oz oyster mushrooms, ¼ cup red Cheshire cheese (may substitute Parmigiano-Reggiano), ⅓ cup butter, ½ lb ground meat (half beef, half pork), ⅔ cup beef stock, Salt, Freshly ground black pepper, 1½ tbs flour, 1 cup milk, 2 tsp curry powder, ½ tsp cayenne pepper, 1 egg yolk, ¼ cup heavy cream, Butter for the gratin dish

Preheat oven to 350°F. Clean mushrooms with a mushroom brush or paper towel, remove hard portions, and cut into narrow strips. Grate cheese coarsely. In a pan, heat half the butter and brown ground meat until crumbly. Add mushrooms and sauté. Add stock and stir. Season with salt and pepper.

In a small saucepan, melt remaining butter, dust with flour, and stir. Gradually add milk, while stirring constantly to make a roux. Add curry powder and season with salt and cayenne. Whisk together egg yolk and cream and fold into the sauce with a wire whisk.

Transfer mushroom-meat mixture to a greased gratin dish. Pour curry sauce over the top. Sprinkle with cheese and brown in the oven for 10 minutes.

 Cheshire is a common English cheese. It is supposedly the oldest cheese produced in England. Its typical color is orangish-yellow. It is made from cow's milk, very hard, and has an intense, salty flavor.

Pork Tenderloin with Mushrooms

1 pork tenderloin (about 1 lb), Salt, Freshly ground black pepper,
4 onions, ¼ cup butter, 10½ oz white mushrooms (or other types),
⅔ cup sour cream, ½ bunch chives

Preheat oven to 350°F. Season pork tenderloin on all sides with salt and pepper. Peel onions and cut into rings. In a pan, heat 1½ tbs butter and brown meat on all sides. In a roasting pan, melt another 1½ tbs butter and place tenderloin inside. Distribute onions around the meat. Add a little water and roast in the oven for about 30 minutes, occasionally adding more water.

Clean mushrooms with a mushroom brush or paper towel, trim, slice larger mushrooms, and leave smaller ones whole. In a pan, heat remaining butter and brown mushrooms on all sides. Five minutes before the tenderloin is done, remove roasting pan from oven, add sour cream and browned mushrooms to meat juices, and stir carefully. Return to the oven and cook tenderloin for another 5 minutes until done. Rinse chives, pat dry, and chop. Arrange tenderloin on a warm platter with onions, mushrooms, and sauce. Garnish with chopped chives.

 This fine Sunday dinner goes well with potato dumplings and a green salad.

Pork Medallions with Sour Cherries and Chanterelles

10½ oz fresh chanterelle mushrooms, 1 green onion,
⅔ cup sour cherries, 1 lb pork tenderloin, 3 tbs butter, ½ tsp herb salt,
Salt, Freshly ground black pepper, 3 tbs canola oil,
3 tbs cherry brandy, 1 pinch cardamom

Clean mushrooms with a mushroom brush or paper towel, trim, and cut in half, if necessary. Clean green onion and chop into fine rings. Rinse cherries, pat dry, remove pits, and cut in half. Cut tenderloin into medallions, the thickness of a thumb.

In a pan, heat 1 tbs butter until very hot and sauté medallions on both sides for about 4 minutes. Remove from the pan, sprinkle lightly with herb salt, cover with aluminum foil, and keep warm. Melt remaining butter in the pan, sauté green onion and mushrooms on all sides, and season with salt and pepper. Keep warm with the meat. Heat canola oil in the pan and braise cherries on all sides. Add cherry brandy and season to taste with cardamom and pepper. Arrange medallions and mushrooms on large plates and top with cherries. Serve with a crusty baguette, polenta, or rice.

Jägerschnitzel

1 oz dried boletus mushrooms, 1⅔ cups mushroom stock,
2 small onions, 14 oz white mushrooms, ½ bunch parsley,
4 veal cutlets (⅓ lb each), Salt, Freshly ground white pepper,
⅓ cup oil, ¼ cup Madeira, ⅔ cup crème fraîche, Parsley

Soak dried mushrooms in hot stock for 30 minutes. Peel and dice onions. Clean white mushrooms with a mushroom brush or paper towel, trim, and slice. Rinse parsley, pat dry, remove leaves from stems, and chop.

Season veal cutlets on both sides with salt and pepper. In a pan, heat oil and sauté veal for about 3 minutes on each side. Remove from pan, cover, and keep warm. Braise onion in pan residues. Remove boletus mushrooms from stock (save the stock), drain, and cut into small pieces. Add all mushrooms to the pan and braise for several minutes. Add stock and reduce for several minutes. Season liberally with Madeira, salt, and pepper. Stir in crème fraîche and reduce slightly. Arrange meat on plates, pour mushroom sauce over the top, and serve sprinkled with parsley

Jägerschnitzel is a classic that belongs in every mushroom cookbook. The use of Madeira makes this version a little different. Serve with spätzle or ribbon pasta.

Zurich-Style Geschnetzeltes

4 veal cutlets (⅓ lb each), 1 yellow onion,
7 oz white mushrooms, 1 bunch curly-leaved parsley,
⅓ cup butter, ¼ cup dry white wine, ¾ cup heavy cream,
Salt, Freshly ground white pepper

Cut veal in half lengthwise and then crosswise against the grain into strips about ½-inch wide. Peel and dice onion. Clean mushrooms with a mushroom brush or paper towel, trim, and slice. Rinse parsley, pat dry, remove leaves from stems, and chop. In a pan, melt half the butter and brown veal in batches. Remove from pan, cover with aluminum foil, and keep warm. Melt remaining butter in the pan and braise onion until translucent. Add mushrooms and sauté. Add wine and cream. Reduce slightly while stirring. Return meat to the pan and stir. Season with salt and pepper. Arrange on warm plates and garnish with chopped parsley.

Traditionally, this dish is served with potato rösti. It is quick to make and everybody loves it, especially children.

Hubertus-Style Veal

⅔ cup chestnuts, 5 large potatoes, 2¼ lb veal loin roast,
Salt, Freshly ground white pepper, 3 tbs oil,
1⅔ cups veal stock, 2 stalks rosemary, 10½ oz boletus mushrooms,
10½ oz chanterelle mushrooms, 1 onion, 1 clove garlic, ¼ cup butter

Preheat oven to 350°F. Using a sharp knife, cut an X through the shell of the chestnuts, place on a baking sheet, and bake in the oven until the shells are easy to remove (15–20 minutes). Cool, remove from shells, and chop finely. Peel potatoes, rinse, and cut into pieces with edges about 1½-inches long.

Turn oven up to 400°F. Salt and pepper veal on all sides. In a roasting pan, heat oil then brown veal on all sides. Add stock, place potatoes around the meat, add rinsed rosemary stalks, cover, and roast in the oven for about 40 minutes.

Clean mushrooms with a mushroom brush or paper towel, trim, and cut into bite-sized pieces. Peel onion and garlic and cut into thin slices. In a pan, heat butter then braise mushrooms, chestnuts, onion, and garlic for 5–7 minutes. Season with salt and pepper.

When finished cooking, remove veal from roasting pan, slice, and arrange on a warm platter. Surround with mushrooms, chestnuts, and potatoes.

Alsatian Veal Fricassee with Slippery Jack Mushrooms

1⅔ lb veal, 1 onion, 4 whole cloves, 2 small carrots,
3 stalks curly-leaved parsley, 2 stalks thyme, 2 bay leaves,
9 oz slippery jack mushrooms, Salt, Freshly ground white pepper,
2 tbs butter, 2 tbs flour, ½ cup dry white wine, 1 egg yolk,
¼ cup crème fraîche, Juice of 1 lemon, Worcestershire sauce (optional)

Cut veal into pieces with edges about ¾-inch long. Peel onion and cut in half. Dice one half finely and stud the other half with cloves. Clean carrots and dice finely. Rinse parsley and thyme, pat dry. Wrap parsley, thyme, and bay leaves in a cheese-cloth pouch. Using a kitchen knife, peel mushroom caps. Then clean with a mushroom brush or paper towel, trim, and cut into quarters.

In a saucepan, melt butter and lightly brown meat in batches, while stirring constantly. Add diced onion and carrots and braise. Season with salt and pepper. Dust with flour, stir, add wine, and ⅔ cup water. Add cheesecloth pouch and studded onion. Cover and simmer for about 40 minutes. Remove cheesecloth and onion. Add mushrooms. Simmer for another 15 minutes. Combine egg yolk, crème fraîche, and lemon juice in a bowl. Season with salt and pepper and let stand for several minutes. Remove meat and mushrooms from saucepan, transfer to a terrine, and keep warm. Spoon egg yolk-crème fraîche and lemon juice mixture into the pan. Do not return to a boil. Season to taste with salt, pepper, and Worcestershire sauce. Pour over fricassee and serve immediately.

The traditional side dish served with this fricassee is buttered rice. However, you can also serve it with wild rice or with peas.

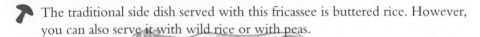

Stewed Rabbit with Chanterelles and White Mushrooms

1 rabbit (about 4½ lb), Salt,
Freshly ground white pepper, 4 carrots, ¼ celery root,
1 parsley root, 3 small onions, 2 cloves garlic,
1 stalk rosemary, ¼ cup butter, 3 tbs tomato paste,
1 bay leaf, 4 cups game stock (chicken stock can be substituted),
9 oz chanterelle mushrooms, 9 oz small white mushrooms,
Herb salt, ½ cup crème fraîche

Preheat oven to 250°F. Rinse rabbit and cut into pieces, pat dry, and rub all over with salt and pepper. Clean carrots, celery root, parsley root, and dice. Peel onions and garlic and cut into thin slices. Rinse rosemary, pat dry, strip leaves from stems, and chop coarsely.

In a roasting pan, melt 2 tbs butter and brown rabbit pieces. Distribute diced vegetables, onions, and garlic among the pieces of meat. Spread half the tomato paste onto the top of the rabbit pieces. Add rosemary and bay leaf, cover, and roast in the oven on the middle rack for 40 minutes. Turn rabbit pieces occasionally, spreading the other side with tomato paste. Gradually add stock and continue roasting (set aside ½ cup stock for the sauce). Clean mushrooms with a mushroom brush or paper towel and trim. In a pan, melt remaining butter and sauté all the mushrooms for about 5 minutes. Season with herb salt and pepper. Remove from pan and keep warm.

When the meat is done, remove it from the roasting pan, cover, and keep warm. Remove bay leaf and put vegetables through a strainer. In a saucepan, combine crème fraîche and remaining stock to form a creamy sauce. Pour sauce over the rabbit and vegetables, coating all sides. Arrange on warm plates and serve with sautéed mushrooms.

 Delicious with a hearty side dish of fried potatoes or croquettes.

Chicken Breast with Mushrooms, White Wine, and Fresh Herbs

4 oz honey mushrooms, 4 oz bay boletes,
1 handful fresh horn of plenty mushrooms (may substitute dried),
2 cloves garlic, 3 stalks fresh thyme, 2 stalks rosemary,
2 chicken breast fillets, ½ cup fruity white wine,
¾ cup heavy cream, 3 tbs butter , Salt, Freshly ground white pepper

Clean mushrooms with a mushroom brush or paper towel, trim, cut in half, and place in a large bowl (do not soak dried horn of plenty mushrooms). Peel garlic and using a sharp knife, cut into paper-thin slices and mix into mushrooms. Rinse thyme and rosemary, pat dry, and strip leaves from stems. Rinse chicken breast fillets and pat dry.

Preheat oven to 450°F. On a baking sheet, spread a double layer of aluminum foil, bend the edges upward 2–3 inches, and seal the corners. Spread mushroom-garlic mixture on the foil, place chicken fillets on top, sprinkle with herbs, and add wine and cream. Cut butter into pieces and top with butter and season with salt and pepper. Cover with a large sheet of aluminum foil and seal the edges. Bake in the oven for 20–25 minutes.

 Italians love to serve this with plain, diamond-shaped pieces of polenta that have been tossed in warm, foamy butter.

Chicken Curry with Asian Mushrooms and Coconut Milk

1 handful dried wood ear mushrooms,
2 oz fresh shiitake mushrooms (may substitute 1 handful dried),
5 large tomatoes, 2 large white onions, 1 inch fresh ginger root,
1 green chile pepper, 4 chicken breast fillets, 3 tbs butter,
1 tsp mustard seeds, 1 handful fenugreek sprouts (Asian market),
1 handful curry leaves (Asian market;
may substitute 1½ tsp Indian curry powder),
1⅔ cups canned coconut milk, 3⅓ cups lukewarm water,
½ tsp coriander, Salt

Pour hot water over wood ear mushrooms and soak for 15 minutes. Drain and chop coarsely. Clean shiitakes with a mushroom brush or paper towel, trim, and cut in half. Cut an X through the skin of the tomatoes, blanch, peel, remove cores, and dice. Peel onions, cut in half, and slice. Peel ginger root and grate coarsely. Cut green chile pepper into rings, removing seeds. Rinse chicken breast fillets, pat dry, and cut into strips the width of a finger.

In a pan, heat butter, add mustard seeds, and stir until the heat causes them to burst. Add fenugreek, onions, ginger, chile pepper, curry leaves, and chopped wood ear mushrooms. Brown well on all sides. After 5 minutes, add chicken and shiitakes. Sauté for another 5 minutes. Add diced tomatoes, coconut milk, and warm water. Continue simmering over medium heat for 10 minutes. Season with coriander and salt to taste.

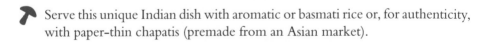 Serve this unique Indian dish with aromatic or basmati rice or, for authenticity, with paper-thin chapatis (premade from an Asian market).

Barbary Duck Breast with Mushrooms and Ginger

*28 oz assorted mushrooms (e.g., chanterelle, field, bay boletes, horn of plenty),
2 onions, ¾ inch fresh ginger root, 3–4 stalks lemon thyme,
1¼ cups Madeira, ¼ cup pumpkin seed oil, ½ cup balsamic vinegar,
1 dried chile pepper, 1½ tsp cloves, 1 tsp allspice, 3 tbs Grappa,
Freshly ground black pepper, 2 Barbary duck breasts,
Oil for sautéing, Cilantro*

On the day before, clean the mushrooms with a mushroom brush or paper towel, trim, and cut into bite-sized pieces. Peel onions and dice. Peel half the ginger and dice coarsely. Rinse lemon thyme and pat dry. In a saucepan, combine Madeira, pumpkin seed oil, and balsamic vinegar. Add onions, ginger, lemon thyme sprigs, chile pepper, 1 tsp cloves, and 1 tsp allspice. Bring to a boil. Simmer mushrooms in this liquid in batches. Remove, transfer to a bowl, and pour liquid over the top.

Peel remaining ginger and mince. Combine ginger, Grappa, pepper, and remaining cloves to make a marinade. Rinse duck breasts, pat dry, and dredge in marinade. Line a casserole dish with aluminum foil, place duck breasts inside, and drizzle remaining marinade over the top. Marinate duck breasts and mushrooms overnight in the refrigerator.

On the following day, preheat oven to 175°F. In a roasting pan, heat oil. Remove duck from the marinade and sear on all sides. Place roasting pan in the oven and depending on the size and desired consistency, roast duck breasts for 1½–2 hours. Drain marinated mushrooms and slice meat. Arrange duck and mushrooms on plates and garnish with a little cilantro.

Venison Wrapped in Chanterelle Crêpes

For the venison: 3⅓ lb saddle of venison,
Salt, Freshly ground white pepper, ¼ cup oil, 1 tbs butter
For the sauce: Bones, skin and sinews from venison,
½ cup each of carrots, leeks, and celery, 1 small onion, 2 tbs oil,
½ cup port wine, ½ cup red wine, 6 cups veal stock, 2 tbs ice-cold butter
For the crêpes: ½ cup flour, ¼ cup butter, 4 eggs, ½ cup water,
1 cup milk, Salt, Butter for frying
For the filling: 4 shallots, 14 oz chanterelle mushrooms,
3 tbs butter, Salt, Freshly ground pepper, 1 bunch parsley,
⅓ lb cooked chicken breast (well chilled), ⅓ cup ice-cold heavy cream
For the garnish: 9 oz small chanterelle mushrooms,
1 tbs butter, Salt, Freshly ground pepper
Plus: Butter for the aluminum foil

Rinse venison, pat dry, and place on a work surface with the meat side down. Using a sharp knife, cut away tenderloins from either side of the backbone. Turn venison over and with a sharp knife, remove sinews, and skin and carefully remove the 2 long backstraps located on either side of the bones. Set aside bones. Season backstraps and tenderloins with salt and pepper. In a pan, heat oil and butter. Brown meat on all sides and let cool.

For the sauce: Chop venison bones into walnut-sized pieces. Peel carrots, clean leek and celery, and dice. Peel onion and chop. In a pan, heat oil and sear bones, skin, and sinews. Add vegetables and sauté until they start to brown. Add port, red wine, and stock. Simmer over low heat for about 4 hours, occasionally skimming off the scum that forms on the top. Pour sauce through a cloth and continue reducing.

For the crêpes: Mix all ingredients thoroughly to form a runny batter and let stand for 15 minutes. In a nonstick pan with very little butter, fry 4–6 paper-thin crêpes (as far as possible, not browned!). Remove and let cool.

For the filling: Peel and dice shallots. Clean chanterelles with a mushroom brush or paper towel, trim, and chop finely. In a pan, melt butter then braise shallots. Add mushrooms, salt lightly, season with pepper, and simmer until all the liquid has evaporated. Remove from heat and let cool. Rinse parsley, pat dry, remove leaves from stems, and chop finely. Dice poultry meat, season with salt, and pepper. Purée in a blender while gradually adding ice-cold cream to form a creamy mixture. Stir in mushrooms and parsley.

Preheat oven to 320°F. Lay out prepared crêpes on a work surface and spread each crêpe with a thin layer of filling. Place 1 piece of meat on each crêpe and roll up. Tightly wrap each rolled crêpe in a piece of buttered aluminum foil. Bake in the hot oven for about 15 minutes, remove, and let stand for several minutes before removing foil.

For the garnish: Clean small chanterelles with a mushroom brush or paper towel and trim. In a pan, heat butter then sauté mushrooms until golden-brown. Season with salt and pepper. Just before serving, cut ice-cold butter into pieces and stir into the reduced sauce. Place each crêpe on a warm plate, pour sauce over the top, and garnish with chanterelles.

French Rice Casserole with Tuna and Bay Boletes

²⁄₃ cup long-grain rice, 1 pinch salt,
9 oz bay boletes (may substitute cremini mushrooms),
4 large beefsteak tomatoes, 1¹⁄₃ cups canned tuna,
¹⁄₄ cup butter, 2–3 tbs flour, 1 cup canned fish stock,
Salt, Freshly ground white pepper, ¹⁄₃ cup heavy cream,
¹⁄₂ cup grated Gruyère (or substitute tangy Emmenthaler),
¹⁄₄ cup dry white wine, Butter for the casserole dish

Prepare rice in salted water according to package directions. Preheat oven to 350°F. Clean mushrooms with a mushroom brush or paper towel, trim, and slice. Cut an X through the skin of the tomatoes, blanch, peel, remove cores, and dice. Drain tuna. In a saucepan, melt butter, sift flour over the top, and stir. Add fish stock and make a roux. Season with salt and pepper. Add cream and gradually fold in cheese. Add wine and stir to form a smooth, creamy sauce.

In a greased casserole dish, arrange layers of rice, mushrooms, tomatoes, and tuna. Pour sauce over the top and bake in the oven on the middle rack for 30 minutes until golden.

This delicious casserole tastes best served with a bowl of crisp tossed salad.

Monkfish with Shiitake Mushrooms and Fresh Ginger

⅓ lb monkfish fillet, Juice of ½ lime, 1 small red chile pepper,
1 clove garlic, ¾ inch fresh ginger root, 1¾ cups white cabbage,
2 oz fresh shiitake mushrooms, ¼ cup soy oil, Herb salt,
Freshly ground white pepper, 1 cup fish stock,
2–3 tbs soy sauce, 1 tsp sesame oil

Rinse fish fillet, pat dry, drizzle with lime juice, and let stand. Cut chile pepper in half, remove stem, seeds and interiors, and chop very finely. Peel garlic and ginger and dice finely. Clean white cabbage, remove core, and cut into strips 1½-inches wide. Clean shiitakes with a mushroom brush or paper towel, trim, and cut into thin slices.

In a pan, heat 2 tbs soy oil then brown fish on both sides (about 2 minutes). Season with herb salt and pepper. Remove from pan, cover with aluminum foil, and keep warm. Heat remaining oil and braise shiitakes, chile pepper, garlic, and ginger until translucent. Add cabbage, cover, and braise over medium heat for 20 minutes. Add stock and season with soy sauce. Transfer mushroom-cabbage mixture to warm plates. Return fish to the pan, flip once and remove. Place fish on top of the vegetables. Drizzle with sesame oil and serve immediately.

 This elegant dish is especially tasty with a side dish of jasmine or aromatic rice.

SAVORY PASTRIES
& QUICHES

Ham Mushroom Croissants

11 oz puff pastry dough (from the supermarket's refrigerated section),
4 oz white mushrooms, 1½ oz ham, 2 tbs chopped parsley,
1 tbs butter, 2 tbs crème fraîche, 1 tbs Dijon mustard,
Salt, Freshly ground white pepper, 1 egg yolk

Preheat oven to 400°F. Cut puff pastry dough into 8–10 equal-sized triangles. Clean mushrooms with a mushroom brush or paper towel, trim, and dice finely. Finely dice ham. Rinse parsley, pat dry, remove leaves from stems, and chop finely. In a pan, melt butter then braise mushrooms for about 3 minutes. Remove from pan and let cool. Combine mushrooms, ham, parsley, crème fraîche, and mustard; stir well. Season with salt and pepper. Distribute this mixture on the puff pastry triangles and roll them up starting from the longest side. Rinse a baking sheet with cold water, place pastries on top, and brush with whisked egg yolk. Bake for about 12 minutes until golden.

 These croissants are a fantastic treat to serve for brunch or breakfast.

Boletus Mushroom Quiche

For the dough: ⅔ cup flour, 1 pinch salt, 1 egg, ⅓ cup cold butter
For the filling: 1 onion, 5 oz boletus mushrooms, ⅔ cup ham,
1 bunch Italian parsley, 1 bunch chives, 1 cup Emmenthaler,
2 tbs butter, Salt, Freshly ground black pepper,
⅔ cup crème fraîche, 2 eggs, 1 pinch freshly grated nutmeg
Plus: Flour for the work surface, Butter for the pan

For the dough: Sift flour into a bowl and form a well in the center. Place salt, egg, and butter cut into pieces in the well and quickly knead into a smooth dough. Wrap in plastic wrap and refrigerate for at least 30 minutes.

For the filling: Peel and dice onion. Clean mushrooms with a mushroom brush or paper towel, trim, and cut into strips. Dice ham finely. Rinse parsley, pat dry, remove leaves from stems, and chop. Rinse chives, pat dry, and chop into fine rings. Grate Emmenthaler coarsely.

Preheat oven to 350°F. In a large pan, melt butter and braise onion until translucent. Add mushrooms and ham, parsley and chives, and season with salt and pepper. Simmer mixture for 3 minutes, while stirring. Remove from pan and let cool. Whisk together crème fraîche and eggs. Add cheese and carefully fold into the mushroom-ham mixture. Season with salt, pepper, and nutmeg.

On a floured surface, roll out dough into a thin sheet and transfer to a greased 11-inch springform pan, forming a border about ¾-inches high around the sides. Pierce bottom several times with a fork. Pour mushroom filling into the pan and bake in the oven on the middle rack for 45 minutes.

 This solid, hearty quiche is ideal for outdoor picnics or as part of a brunch.

Puff Pastry Tart with Assorted Mushrooms

8–9 oz puff pastry dough (from the supermarket's refrigerated section),
Flour for the work surface, Butter for the pan, 1 onion,
1 clove garlic, ¼ cup ham, 9 oz assorted mushrooms,
1 small leek, ¼ cup canola oil, Salt, Freshly ground pepper,
⅓ cup heavy cream, 2 eggs, Freshly grated nutmeg,
Cardamom, 2 tbs grated Emmenthaler

Preheat oven to 400°F. Roll out puff pastry dough on a floured work surface and transfer to a greased 11-inch springform pan, forming a high border around the sides. Pierce bottom several times with a fork.

Peel onion and garlic and dice finely. Dice ham. Clean mushrooms with a mushroom brush or paper towel, trim, and slice. Clean leek, rinse thoroughly, and chop into fine rings. In a pan, heat 2 tbs canola oil and braise onion and garlic. Add ham, mushrooms and leek, and sauté. Season with salt and pepper. Pour into springform pan.

Whisk together cream and eggs. Season with salt, pepper, nutmeg, and cardamom. Pour egg cream over the mushrooms and sprinkle with cheese. Bake in the oven on the middle rack for about 20 minutes.

 This tart goes with a crispy green salad.

Puff Pastry Tart with Shrimp and Mushrooms

12 oz puff pastry dough (from the supermarket's refrigerated section),
7 oz assorted mushrooms, ½ cup white wine,
½ cup vegetable stock, ⅓ lb peeled shrimp, 1 onion,
2 tbs butter, 1 tbs flour, ¼ cup sour cream, 2 tsp lemon juice,
Salt, Freshly ground white pepper or a little cayenne pepper, ½ bunch parsley

Preheat oven to 400°F. Roll out puff pastry dough on a floured work surface, cut out a circle with a 10-inch diameter, and transfer to a baking sheet lined with parchment paper. From the remaining dough, cut out small circles (1-inch diameter) and place them in an overlapping pattern around the edges of the dough (this way, the edges will rise during baking). Pierce dough several times with a fork. Bake in the oven for about 25 minutes until golden.

Clean mushrooms with a mushroom brush or paper towel, trim, and chop. In a saucepan, heat white wine and vegetable stock. Simmer mushrooms and shrimp separately in the hot stock for 3–4 minutes each, remove, and set aside. Peel and dice onion. In a pan, melt butter then braise onion until translucent. Stir in flour. Gradually add mushroom-shrimp liquid and bring to a boil while stirring. The sauce shouldn't be too runny. If necessary, reduce slightly over low heat. Stir in sour cream. Add mushrooms and shrimp. Season with lemon juice, salt, and white or cayenne pepper. Rinse parsley, pat dry, remove leaves from stems, and chop. Spoon mushroom-shrimp mixture on the finished pastry shell and garnish with parsley.

 Serve with a green salad and white wine. Seafood and mushrooms go very well together. Be creative with this recipe and try out the many possible combinations!

Chanterelle Tart with Fresh Herbs, Spinach, and Pecorino

2 small cloves garlic, 1 small onion, 16 oz chanterelle mushrooms,
½ cup pecorino cheese, 2 stale rolls,
2 stalks each of basil, thyme, Italian parsley, oregano, and marjoram,
1 lb spinach, 3 tbs extra-virgin olive oil, 2 tbs butter,
Salt, Freshly ground black pepper,
14–16 oz puff pastry dough (from the supermarket's refrigerated section),
2 cups ricotta cheese, 5 eggs, 1 pinch freshly grated nutmeg, 1 egg yolk for brushing

Peel garlic and onion and mince. Clean mushrooms with a mushroom brush or paper towel, trim, and cut into small pieces. Grate pecorino finely. Cut rolls into small cubes. Rinse herbs, pat dry, remove leaves from stems, and chop coarsely. Rinse spinach thoroughly, clean, and drain.

In a pan, heat olive oil and braise garlic, onion, and mushrooms. Set aside and let cool slightly. In a tall pot, melt butter with 1 tsp salt and braise spinach over medium heat for about 4 minutes. Remove from the pot, let cool, thoroughly squeeze out liquid, chop coarsely, and season with pepper.

Preheat oven to 350°F. Rinse a 11-inch pie or springform pan with cold water and line with a sheet of puff pastry dough so that the edges hang slightly over the sides. In a large bowl, combine mushrooms, spinach, ricotta, herbs, and grated cheese. Thoroughly stir in eggs. Season with salt, pepper, and nutmeg. Spread half this mixture into the pastry shell. Cut out another sheet of puff pastry dough so it fits as a middle layer for the mushroom-vegetable mixture. Spread on the other half of the mixture and fold the overhanging edges of the dough inward. Bake in the oven for 55–60 minutes until golden, brushing the surface with whisked egg yolk several times.

Small Mushroom Gratins with Anise

10½ oz large white mushrooms, Butter for the gratin dishes,
4 eggs, ⅓ cup heavy cream, ½ tsp anise,
3 tsp chopped Italian parsley, Herb salt, Freshly ground black pepper

Preheat oven to 400°F. Clean mushrooms with a mushroom brush or paper towel, trim, and cut into thick slices. Grease 4-6 individual gratin dishes and spoon mushrooms evenly inside. Combine eggs, cream, anise, and parsley. Season with herb salt and pepper. Pour egg cream over the mushrooms and bake gratins in the oven on the top rack for 15–20 minutes.

These little mushroom gratins are excellent for a brunch or breakfast buffet.

Calzone—Tasty Stuffed Pizza Pockets

For the dough: 1 tbs fresh yeast, ½ tsp sugar,
1 cup lukewarm water, 1 cup white flour,
2 tbs extra-virgin olive oil, 1 pinch salt
For the filling: 4 oz cremini mushrooms,
2 stalks fresh or 1 tsp dried oregano,
¼ cup Parmigiano-Reggiano, 1 mozzarella ball, 4 slices ham,
⅔ cup ricotta cheese, 2 eggs, Salt, Freshly ground pepper
Plus: Flour for the work surface, Olive oil, 1 egg yolk for brushing

For the dough: Combine yeast, sugar, 2 tbs water, and 2 tbs flour. Stir until smooth to form a pre-dough. Cover and let rise for 30 minutes. Sift remaining flour into a bowl and form a well in the center. Pour in pre-dough, drizzle in olive oil, add salt and remaining water, and process into a workable dough. Knead dough vigorously until bubbles form, then shape into a ball, cover, and let rise in a warm place for another 30 minutes. Preheat oven to 425°F.

For the filling: Clean mushrooms with a mushroom brush or paper towel, trim, and cut into thin slices. Rinse fresh oregano, pat dry, remove leaves from stems, and chop. Grate Parmigiano-Reggiano coarsely and dice mozzarella finely. Cut ham into fine strips. Combine ricotta, eggs, mushrooms, Parmigiano-Reggiano, mozzarella, and ham. Season with salt, pepper, and oregano.

Cut dough in half then knead both halves again. On a floured surface, roll out each half into a circle with a diameter of about 11 inches. Brush each sheet with a thin coating of olive oil and spoon mushroom cheese mixture over half of each, leaving ¾ inches border free around the edges. Fold over the other half, fold the edges of the dough inward slightly, and press firmly together. Place both calzone on a baking sheet lined with parchment paper and bake in the oven for 5 minutes. Remove, brush the surfaces with egg yolk whisked in a little olive oil, and continue baking for 20 minutes until done.

Pizza with Porcini, Arugula, and Serrano Ham

For the dough: 2 cups flour, 1 cube fresh yeast, 1 pinch salt,
1 pinch sugar, 1½ cups lukewarm water, 3 tbs olive oil
For the topping: 1 onion, 3 cloves garlic, 2 tbs extra-virgin olive oil,
1½ cups canned peeled tomatoes, 2 medium porcini (about 9 oz),
⅔ cup arugula, 3 stalks basil, Salt, Freshly ground pepper,
⅔ cup mascarpone cheese, 3 tbs truffle oil,
2 mozzarella balls, 8 thin slices Serrano ham
Plus: Flour for the work surface, Butter for the baking sheet

For the dough: Sift flour into a bowl and make a well in the center. Dissolve yeast, salt and sugar in lukewarm water, and pour into the well. Add olive oil and knead all ingredients into a workable dough. Cover and let rise in a warm place for at least 30 minutes.

For the topping: Peel onion and garlic and mince. In a pan, heat olive oil and braise onion and garlic. Add tomatoes and reduce for about 10 minutes.

Clean mushrooms with a mushroom brush or paper towel, trim, and cut into thin slices. Rinse arugula and basil, pat dry, remove stems, and chop coarsely. Add herbs to tomato sauce and season with salt and pepper. Stir together mascarpone and truffle oil until smooth. Cut mozzarella into thin slices. Preheat oven to 350°F.

On a floured surface, roll out dough into a thin sheet and transfer to a greased baking sheet. Spread with tomato sauce, and top with mushrooms and mozzarella. Place dollops of mascarpone on top. Bake in the oven on the middle rack for about 15 minutes. Add Serrano ham on top of the hot pizza and serve immediately.

Gorgonzola Pizza

For the dough: 2 cups flour, 1 cube fresh yeast, 1 pinch salt,
1 pinch sugar, 1½ cups lukewarm water, 3 tbs olive oil
For the topping: 1 onion, 2 cloves garlic, 2 stalks oregano,
2 stalks basil, 2 tbs extra-virgin olive oil,
1¼ cups canned strained tomatoes, Salt,
Freshly ground black pepper, 5 oz white mushrooms,
⅔ cup Gorgonzola, ⅔ cup sliced salami
Plus: Flour for the work surface, Butter for the baking sheet

For the dough: Sift flour into a bowl and make a well in the center. Dissolve yeast, salt, and sugar in lukewarm water; pour into the well and knead together with flour and olive oil to form a workable dough. Cover and let rise in a warm place for at least 30 minutes.

For the topping: Peel onion and garlic and mince. Rinse herbs, pat dry, remove leaves from stems, and cut into strips. Combine olive oil, tomatoes, and herbs. Season with salt and pepper. Clean mushrooms with a mushroom brush or paper towel, trim, and cut into thin slices. Finely dice Gorgonzola. Preheat oven to 400°F. Roll out dough on a floured surface and transfer to a greased baking sheet. Spread with tomato sauce, and then top with mushrooms and salami slices. Sprinkle Gorgonzola over the top. Bake in the oven on the middle rack for 15–20 minutes.

Try replacing the Gorgonzola with another tangy cheese. This pizza tastes heavenly with Gruyère. For this version, however, fresh rosemary leaves taste better than oregano.

PRESERVING MUSHROOMS

Dried Mushrooms

Use only unblemished mushrooms (e.g., horn of plenty, boletus, parasol) without bruises or mold. Clean mushrooms carefully with a mushroom brush or paper towel and trim. Cut into slices ¼-inch thick, distribute on a baking sheet covered with paper towels, and dry in a 125°F oven with the door cracked open, turning several times in the process. Or, thread the mushroom slices onto strings and hang them in a warm, dry place. Place the completely dried mushrooms (they must be bone dry) in clean, dry jelly jars and seal.

Boletus mushrooms quickly become tough and develop a slightly bitter flavor. Shiitake and wood ear mushrooms are generally already dried. Soak dried mushrooms in hot water and use them immediately, or else crush them in a mortar and use the powdered mushrooms for seasoning soups and sauces.

Truffle Oil

2–3 tbs sliced black truffles, ½ tsp freshly ground sea salt,
3 cups extra-virgin olive oil

Sprinkle truffle shavings with sea salt and let stand. In a small sauce pan, heat some of the olive oil. Toss the truffles in the oil, remove from heat, and let stand for another 10 minutes. Transfer truffles, including oil, to clean, dry, dark-glass, wide-mouth bottles and slowly add remaining olive oil. Seal bottles well and store in a cool, dark place for 4 weeks.

Always heat truffle oil when you use it to release its wonderful aroma.

Boletus Mushrooms in Oil

1 small clove garlic, ½ bunch Italian parsley,
3–4 medium boletus mushrooms, 1 tsp freshly ground sea salt,
4 cups extra-virgin olive oil

Peel garlic and cut into paper-thin slices with a truffle slicer or very sharp knife. Rinse parsley, pat thoroughly dry, remove leaves from stems, and chop finely. Clean mushrooms with a mushroom brush or paper towel, trim, and cut into small cubes. In a bowl, combine garlic and parsley. Stir in mushrooms, sprinkle with sea salt, and let stand for 10 minutes. Transfer mushroom mixture to a large colander and pat dry with paper towels. Return to the bowl, add 4 cups olive oil and stir. Cover and let stand for about 30 minutes. Stir again. Transfer to clean, dry jelly jars and fill up to the screw threads with olive oil. Seal immediately and store in a dark place.

After 2 weeks, the mushrooms will be well marinated. Serve them as an appetizer with fresh ciabatta or a baguette. They are also a delicacy served on top of arugula or frisée lettuce.

Mushroom Oil

1 boletus mushroom (or 5 horn of plenty mushrooms or
10 small honey mushrooms or 1 large parasol mushroom), 1 lemon,
3 white peppercorns, 12–17 cups extra-virgin olive oil

Clean mushrooms with a mushroom brush or paper towels, trim, cut caps into narrow strips, and chop stems coarsely. Rinse lemon under hot water and zest. Place mushrooms and lemon zest in a clean, dry, dark-glass, wide-mouth bottle. Add peppercorns and pour in olive oil. Seal tightly and store in a cool, dark place for 3–4 weeks. Drain oil and pour into another bottle. Use to season salads or pasta.

Truffle Pieces in Madeira

3 oz pieces from 1 small black truffle,
Freshly ground sea salt, 1 pinch cinnamon,
About ½ cup good Madeira

Dust truffle pieces lightly with sea salt and cinnamon and let stand for about 15 minutes. Place in a large, clean, dry jelly jar and pour in enough Madeira to almost cover the truffles. Seal and store in the refrigerator.

Use this aromatic liquid and the truffle pieces to refine sauces. A few shots of this elixir will also give a mushroom cream sauce a unique accent and bring all who taste it under its spell.

Truffle Butter

2 oz canned black truffle pieces, 1 cup softened butter,
⅓ cup good Madeira, Salt, 1 pinch freshly grated nutmeg

Finely chop truffle pieces. In a small pan, heat 2 tbs butter. Toss truffles in butter, add Madeira, and reduce to a syrupy mixture, while stirring constantly. Remove from heat, pour pan contents into a bowl, and work in remaining butter. Continue beating until the mixture becomes creamy. Season with 1 pinch salt and nutmeg. Cool completely before serving.

Marinated Mushrooms

16–18 oz assorted wild mushrooms (e.g., horn of plenty,
chanterelle, scaly tooth, slippery jack, or oyster mushrooms),
½ tsp sesame seeds, ½ tsp fennel seeds, 20 pink peppercorns,
1 tsp coriander seeds, 2 tbs butter, 1 tbs powdered sugar,
3 cups hearty red wine, ⅓–½ cup extra-virgin olive oil, Salt

Clean mushrooms with a mushroom brush or paper towel (first peel caps of slippery jack mushrooms), trim, and cut in half. Cut larger mushrooms into quarters or slice. In a mortar, crush sesame seeds, fennel seeds, pink peppercorns, and coriander seeds.

In a pan, melt butter, sift in powdered sugar, and caramelize. Add red wine and reduce over low heat for about 7 minutes. Heat a little olive oil in another pan and brown mushrooms in batches. In a bowl, combine browned mushrooms, salt, crushed spices, red wine liquid, and a lot of olive oil. Marinate for about 20 minutes. Pour into clean, dry jelly jars, add just enough olive oil to cover the mushrooms, seal tightly, and store in a cool, dark place.

Marinated mushrooms should be consumed within 2 weeks.

Save yourself the trouble of sealing them in jars and serve these delicious mushrooms immediately as a warm appetizer.

Wild Mushroom Pesto with Pine Nuts

2 small cloves garlic, 1 bunch Italian parsley,
3 medium porcinis, 8 fresh morels (or 2 oz dried),
5 bay boletes, 5 horn of plenty mushrooms, 8 cremini mushrooms,
5 slippery jack mushrooms, Freshly ground sea salt,
½ cup pine nuts, 6 cups extra-virgin olive oil

Peel garlic and mince or squeeze through a press. Rinse parsley, pat thoroughly dry, remove leaves from stems, and chop very finely. Clean mushrooms with a mushroom brush or paper towel (first peel caps of slippery jack mushrooms), trim, and mince. In a bowl, combine garlic, parsley, and mushrooms. Sprinkle with sea salt and let stand. Chop pine nuts and add to mushrooms. In a mortar, crush mushroom mixture finely and in batches, while adding olive oil. Transfer this mixture to a large bowl and stir in remaining olive oil (set aside a little to top off the jars). Cover mushroom pesto and let stand for about 30 minutes, and stir again. Pour into clean, dry, jelly jars and fill up to the screw threads with olive oil. Seal immediately and store in a cool, dark place.

Pour pesto over freshly cooked linguini or spaghettini, shave Parmigiano-Reggiano over the top, and in the blink of an eye, you'll have a heavenly pasta dish on the table!

Mushroom Spread

⅔ cup green spelt (available in natural food stores),
3 cups vegetable stock, 2 onions, 2 cloves garlic,
5 oz white mushrooms, 1 bunch parsley, ½ cup softened butter,
1 tsp Truffle Butter (recipe on page 111), 2 tsp Worcestershire sauce,
2–3 tbs Dijon mustard, Ground rosemary,
Sea salt, Freshly ground white pepper

Combine spelt and stock, cover, and simmer over low heat for about 15 minutes. Remove from heat, keep covered, and let stand for 20 minutes. Peel onion and garlic and dice. Clean mushrooms with a mushroom brush or paper towel, trim, and dice. Rinse parsley, pat dry, remove leaves from stems, and chop finely. In a pan, melt 3–4 tbs butter and braise onion and garlic until translucent. Add mushrooms and sauté for about 5 minutes. In a food processor, purée spelt, remaining butter, truffle butter, mushrooms, Worcestershire sauce, mustard, salt and pepper, and transfer to a screw-top jar. This bread spread keeps in the refrigerator for up to 3 days.

LIST OF RECIPES

Soups

Salads

Appetizers & Snacks

Terrines & Soufflés

Rice & Pasta Dishes

Hearty Entrées

Savory Pastries & Quiches

Preserving Mushrooms

●

Index of Mushroom Types